NEW DIRECTIONS FOR COMMUNITY COLLEGES

Arthur M. Cohen
EDITOR-IN-CHIEF

Florence B. Brawer
ASSOCIATE EDITOR

Determining the Economic Benefits of Attending Community College

Jorge R. Sanchez
Frankie Santos Laanan
Coast Community College District

EDITORS

Number 104, Winter 1998

JOSSEY-BASS PUBLISHERS
San Francisco

Clearinghouse for Community Colleges

DETERMINING THE ECONOMIC BENEFITS OF ATTENDING COMMUNITY COLLEGE
Jorge R. Sanchez, Frankie Santos Laanan (eds.)
New Directions for Community Colleges, no. 104
Volume XXVI, number 4
Arthur M. Cohen, Editor-in-Chief
Florence B. Brawer, Associate Editor

New Directions for Community Colleges is indexed in Current Index to Journals in Education (ERIC).

Microfilm copies of issues and articles are available in 16mm and 35mm, as well as microfiche in 105mm, through University Microfilms Inc., 300 North Zeeb Road, Ann Arbor, Michigan 48106–1346.

ISSN 0194-3081   ISBN 0-7879-4237-5

NEW DIRECTIONS FOR COMMUNITY COLLEGES is part of The Jossey-Bass Higher and Adult Education Series and is published quarterly by Jossey-Bass Inc., Publishers, 350 Sansome Street, San Francisco, California 94104–1342, in association with the ERIC Clearinghouse for Community Colleges. Periodicals postage paid at San Francisco, California, and at additional mailing offices. POSTMASTER: Send address changes to New Directions for Community Colleges, Jossey-Bass Inc., Publishers, 350 Sansome Street, San Francisco, California 94104–1342.

SUBSCRIPTIONS cost $57.00 for individuals and $107.00 for institutions, agencies, and libraries. Prices subject to change.

THE MATERIAL in this publication is based on work sponsored wholly or in part by the Office of Educational Research and Improvement, U.S. Department of Education, under contract number RI-93-00-2003. Its contents do not necessarily reflect the views of the Department or any other agency of the U.S. Government.

EDITORIAL CORRESPONDENCE should be sent to the Editor-in-Chief, Arthur M. Cohen, at the ERIC Clearinghouse for Community Colleges, University of California, 3051 Moore Hall, 405 Hilgard Avenue, Los Angeles, California 90095–1521. All manuscripts receive anonymous reviews by external referees.

Cover photograph © Rene Sheret, After Image, Los Angeles, California, 1990.

www.josseybass.com

Printed in the United States of America on acid-free recycled paper containing 100 percent recovered waste paper, of which at least 20 percent is postconsumer waste.

CONTENTS

EDITORS' NOTES   1
Jorge R. Sanchez, Frankie Santos Laanan

1. Economic Benefits of a Community College Education: Issues of   5
Accountability and Performance Measures
Jorge R. Sanchez, Frankie Santos Laanan
New research has emerged on the economic benefits of attending commu-
nity colleges. The authors discuss policy issues relating to accountability
and performance measures.

2. From Performance Reporting to Performance-Based Funding: 17
Florida's Experiences in Workforce Development Performance
Measurement
Jay J. Pfeiffer
In Florida, there is an accountability movement toward providing state
funds to public higher education institutions based on outcome measures.

3. Translating Data into Useful Information and Knowledge   29
Loretta Seppanen
The author summarizes the new knowledge resulting from Washington
State's use of administrative records for outcomes analysis.

4. Collaborative Administrative Record Matching in California   41
W. Charles Wiseley
Since the early 1990s, the California Community Colleges Chancellor's
Office has been involved in student follow-up. The author discusses the
events that led to the creation of the committee of practitioners and raises
policy issues concerning collaboration between agencies.

5. Measurable Outcomes of Workforce Development and the   53
Economic Impact of Attending a North Carolina Community
College
Larry W. Gracie
Workforce preparedness has received much attention in the community col-
lege system. Two outcome measures of successful workforce training are
discussed.

6. Partnering to Identify and Support High-Wage Programs   61
Kae R. Hutchison, Sharon Story Kline, Carol Mandt, Suzanne L. Marks
The authors of this case study describe three separate but related activities
in which wage and job accountability indicators play a key role.

7. Institutional Level Implementation: Translating Research into   69
Current Practice
Fred Carvell, Martha Graham, William E. Piland
This case study describes how wage data are converted for local use in college planning, program improvement, and measurement of institutional effectiveness.

8. Descriptive Analysis of Students' Post-College Earnings from   77
California Community Colleges
Frankie Santos Laanan
The author presents the results of follow-up data of students who last attended a California community college in the 1992–1993 academic year and discusses policy implications.

9. Looking Ahead: A National Measure of Post–Community   89
College Earnings
Jorge R. Sanchez
This chapter addresses the issue of whether a national definition to measure students' post-college earnings is warranted. It presents policy and methodological concerns and discusses recommendations.

10. Employment and Earnings Outcomes: New Perspectives   95
David W. Stevens
The author elaborates on the use of administrative databases and discusses policy implications in the efforts to examine the employment and post-college earnings of students.

11. Sources and Information: Economic Benefits of a   103
Community College Degree
Elizabeth Foote
This chapter provides an annotated bibliography of materials from the ERIC system that highlights previous studies that focus on student follow-up efforts using unemployment insurance wage records and other administrative databases.

INDEX   113

EDITORS' NOTES

Although much has been written about educational attainment and its relationship to individual earnings, most of the evidence is based on the differences between four-year college graduates and high school graduates (Haller, 1982; Henderson and Ottinger, 1985; Pace, 1979). Only recently has a wave of research studies been advanced that has focused on the economic benefits of attending community colleges. Because community colleges serve a variety of functions, the focus of recent research has been to examine the extent to which completing a certificate or associate degree in vocational programs affects students' post-college earnings (Pfeiffer, 1990; Sanchez and Laanan, 1997; Seppanen, 1994).

In the wake of new federal and state legislation, community colleges are faced with demands to provide accountability reports on numerous student outcome measures. One measure that has received attention by policy makers is the question of community colleges' contribution to students' economic worth. That is, how do students, as a result of completing a certificate or an associate degree in a vocational education concentration, benefit in terms of their post-college earnings? Furthermore, what efforts have states engaged in to design a methodology to follow up students?

The objective of this volume is to address the efforts by several states, including California, Florida, North Carolina, and Washington, in following up students to determine economic gains as measured by their post-college earnings. Specifically, this volume includes chapters that address three broad themes: policy, legislation, and accountability; collaboration efforts at the state level; and case studies. Further, the chapters cover the different methodologies employed by these states, the practical uses of the data by vocational education administrators or faculty, and the implications for accountability reporting. This volume is important for community colleges around the country because the chapters provide useful information to faculty, administrators, scholars, and professional practitioners to improve programs.

In Chapter One, we present a review of the literature about the relationship between educational attainment and earnings with an emphasis on the sub-baccalaureate. We explore the current emergence of accountability in community colleges as it relates to the establishment of a performance measure that addresses the benefit of attending a community college.

In Chapter Two, Jay J. Pfeiffer traces Florida's efforts to respond to questions about employment, its relation to training, and other workforce development issues. With the recent passage of legislation, Florida has moved toward a comprehensive application of performance measures. Such measures are tied to performance-based funding in which there is an emphasis on desired outcomes.

In Chapter Three, Loretta Seppanen shares her insights from a decade of experience learning about the outcomes of job preparatory training in the community and technical colleges in Washington state from administrative records. More specifically, Seppanen discusses how data derived from the Data Linking for Outcomes Assessment are translated into information and how this information is translated into knowledge, and examines the kind of choices that are made as data become information.

In Chapter Four, W. Charles Wiseley presents background information about past and current efforts made by the California Community Colleges Chancellor's Office in the use of administrative databases to assess the post-college earnings of students. Wiseley discusses the three core measures for programs funded by the Carl D. Perkins Vocational Education and Applied Technology Act and the state's accountability system.

In Chapter Five, Larry W. Gracie discusses North Carolina's adoption of an expanded mission and goals statement, which reemphasized workforce preparedness in the community college system. In addition to presenting the latest findings, the author discusses two specific outcome measures—employment rates and median annual salary of program completers—and the policy efforts relating to preparing students for workforce training.

In Chapter Six, Kae R. Hutchison, Sharon Story Kline, Carol Mandt, and Suzanne L. Marks present a case study of Bellevue Community College (BCC) and its efforts to become more responsive to business and industry by providing education and training to develop skilled workers. Through partnerships with local companies, BCC has developed innovative ways to respond to the workforce needs of the region and, in particular, to identify high wage programs in emerging technology fields.

In Chapter Seven, Fred Carvell, Martha Graham, and William E. Piland discuss how a college, located in Southern California, utilizes information about students' post-college earnings and the extent to which the information is incorporated and converted for local use. The authors share how the information is used in three areas: college planning, program improvement, and measurement of institutional effectiveness.

In Chapter Eight, Frankie Santos Laanan presents the results of follow-up data of former students from California community colleges who last attended during the 1992–93 academic year. The author highlights the results by age group, selected major fields, and economic status. Policy implications are presented about the use of administrative databases to evaluate the post-college earnings of students.

In Chapter Nine, Jorge R. Sanchez explores the notion of advancing a national definition to measure the post-college earnings of students from community colleges. The author discusses some of the policy and methodological concerns that affect the development and implementation of such a national measure. In Chapter Ten, David W. Stevens offers new perspectives in examining employment and earnings outcome.

The final chapter, by Elizabeth Foote, is devoted to additional sources of previous and current research that provide information about state efforts in the use of administrative databases, performance measures, and accountability issues discussed in this volume.

Jorge R. Sanchez
Frankie Santos Laanan
Editors

References

Haller, A. "Reflections on the Social Psychology of Status Attainment." In R. Hauser, D. Mechanic, A. Haller, and T. Hauser (eds.), *Social Structure and Behavior.* New York: Academic Press, 1982.

Henderson, C., and Ottinger, C. "College Degrees—Still a Ladder to Success?" *Journal of College Placement,* 1985, *45,* 35.

Pace, C. R. *Measuring Outcomes of College: Fifty Years of Findings and Recommendations for the Future.* San Francisco: Jossey-Bass, 1979.

Pfeiffer, J. *Florida Education and Training Placement Program: Annual Report.* Tallahassee: Florida Department of Education, 1990.

Sanchez, J. R., and Laanan, F. S. "The Economic Returns of a Community College Education." *Community College Review,* 1997, 25 (3), 73–87.

Seppanen, L. J. *Job Placement Rates for Graduates of Washington Community and Technical College Vocational Programs.* Research Report No. 94-7. Olympia: Washington State Board for Community and Technical Colleges, 1994. (ED 382 255)

JORGE R. SANCHEZ is director of vocational education and institutional research at Coast Community College District in Costa Mesa, California, and doctoral candidate in higher education at the University of California, Los Angeles.

FRANKIE SANTOS LAANAN is senior research analyst in vocational education and institutional research at Coast Community College District in Costa Mesa, California.

Accountability in community colleges has taken center stage. This chapter focuses on students' post-college earnings as a specific outcome or performance measure. The authors discuss the benefits of a community college education, outline the methodologies used to assess students, and present policy implications of accountability and performance measures.

Economic Benefits of a Community College Education: Issues of Accountability and Performance Measures

Jorge R. Sanchez, Frankie Santos Laanan

The American community college has been the nation's primary site of access to higher education (Cohen and Brawer, 1996; Eaton, 1994; Koltai, 1993). Dougherty (1994, p. 3) asserts that community colleges continue to provide the primary access to a college education in a systematic and cost-effective way. Since its inception, the community college curriculum has offered a variety of services to its constituents, including vocational-technical education, continuing education, remedial education, community service, and academic transfer preparation (Cohen and Brawer, 1996).

Although each function is equally important, one function of community colleges that has received considerable attention from legislators, policy makers, and researchers is that of vocational-technical education. According to Cohen and Brawer (1996, p. 22), the vocational-technical curriculum was written into the earliest educational plans in most states. Such programs are considered *terminal study* because students who pursue this route tend not to continue at a four-year institution. Rather, they seek employment in the field in which they trained. The foundation of vocational-technical or occupational programs is to teach students the essential skills, knowledge, and abilities that link to the world of work.

The success of a system of workforce training for students can be measured in many ways. This chapter focuses on a specific outcome: the economic benefits of a community college education. It is important to emphasize, however, that the post-college earnings of students is one of several outcomes or performance measures that constitute the big picture of institutional effectiveness.

Economic Benefits of Community College Education

A commonly held belief is that formal education has a strong positive association with earnings. Individuals are motivated to pursue and complete an education beyond high school to achieve a higher paying job and a higher position. The "economic benefits" of a community college education could be defined as the amount of money an individual receives from working or the gains in a person's earnings over time. According to the U.S. Department of Labor (1992), workers who have the most education tend to have the highest average annual earnings and the lowest unemployment rates. The focus of research has traditionally been on the benefits of a baccalaureate degree or higher, whereas the value of a two-year education is often overlooked or underestimated.

Background and Review of Literature. In examining the effects of education on individual earnings, most of the research has focused primarily on the comparison between high school graduates and four-year college graduates (Henderson and Ottinger, 1985; Haller, 1982; Adams and Jaffe, 1971). As a result, little is known about the value of an associate degree or vocational certificate from community colleges (Sanchez and Laanan, 1997; Romano, 1986). Most reports show the economic payoffs of obtaining a baccalaureate degree on an individual's average earnings. Data provided by federal agencies like the U.S. Bureau of the Census tend to aggregate educational attainment levels and group students into the following categories: not a high school graduate; high school graduate; some college; baccalaureate, master's, doctoral, or professional degree completers. Included in the "some college" category are all individuals who complete less than a four-year program, including those who attain an associate degree or certificate. Data categorized in this way limit the ability of researchers to isolate the contribution of community colleges in terms of the economic benefit to individuals' post-college earnings (Sanchez and Laanan, 1997; Grubb, 1996; Romano, 1986).

Relationship Between Education and Earnings. There are two popular frameworks to explain the effects of formal education on an individual's earnings. The first is the human capital theory (Becker, 1992), which derives from an economic paradigm and is one of the most popular frameworks scholars have employed. Becker defined *human capital* as the economic effects of investment in education on employment and earnings. The concept of human capital is in all respects analogous to the economist's traditional concept of physical capital. In the lexicon of economists, physical capital includes all useful physical assets (for example, currency, property, precious metals, and jewelry). In education, the term means acquiring the energy, motivation, skills, and knowledge that can be harnessed over time to the task of producing goods and services. In essence, the human capital theory measures the return on investment in oneself.

The second framework is the notion of *certification* or *screening*. That is, employers can use college education as a way to screen the applicant pool or to require a bachelor's degree (or higher) as a way of certifying prospective employees (Jencks et al., 1979). In other words, by virtue of possessing the bachelor's degree, individuals are perceived as meeting a certification that distinguishes them from non–degree recipients, and are therefore rewarded with higher paying jobs or career paths. Arguably, the certification or screening concept is applicable for students who complete an associate degree or vocational certificate as well.

Effects of Community College Education. Students who choose to attend a community college can pursue a variety of objectives ranging from the traditional liberal arts curriculum that will eventually lead to a four-year institution to vocational/occupational programs. Many of the vocational programs provide students the opportunity to obtain a certificate or associate degree in a specific area. Moreover, many of these programs are closely linked to the world of work and consequently students can move into the labor force immediately upon completion of a course of study.

A common finding in the literature is that individuals who begin at a two-year college rather than a four-year college are significantly less likely to complete a bachelor's degree than their four-year counterparts. According to Astin (1985), students who begin their education at a two-year college are less likely to complete a baccalaureate degree because these institutions often have a high proportion of low-income and underprepared students and lack residential facilities, which provide opportunities for student involvement. Critics of community colleges perpetuate the notion that the benefits of attending a two-year institution are limited. The assumption is made that students who achieve less than the baccalaureate degree will find that their education has little positive effect on their current and future earnings potential.

In a recent book, *Working in the Middle: Strengthening Education and Training for the Mid-Skilled Labor Force,* Grubb (1996) offers some context for the ongoing debate among scholars and researchers over the economic value of a community college education. Because the data have been unreliable, he argues that assessing the economic benefits of a sub-baccalaureate education is a continual challenge. Based on the latest findings from the Survey of Income and Program Participation (SIPP), Grubb maintains that whereas individuals with baccalaureate degrees dominate managerial and professional jobs, those who earn an associate degree double their chances of becoming a professional or manager compared to the chances for someone with a high school diploma. Further, he asserts that the chances of obtaining a job requiring technical skills are much better with an associate degree or vocational certificate, and the likelihood of becoming a laborer or having an unskilled position is reduced. In other words, having a sub-baccalaureate credential as well as post-secondary coursework without credentials helps individuals move from the bottom levels of the labor force into mid-skilled positions (p. 87). Some additional findings reported by Grubb (1996) include the following:

Men and women who complete associate degrees and certificates earn more than high school graduates but less than those with baccalaureate degrees. Individuals between the ages of twenty-five and sixty-four in 1987 with associate degrees earned 21.5 percent more than those with high school diplomas, whereas those with vocational certificates earned 14.6 percent more.
Analysis of the economic effects of credentials by field of study shows that economic returns to associate degrees are highest for men in engineering and computer fields, public service (for example, fire fighters, police, some social service workers, and legal aides), and vocational/technical fields (including trades and construction crafts). These economic benefits were significant for all fields in 1987 and for engineering and computer fields in 1990. For women, business and health occupations gave consistently positive economic returns in 1987 and again in 1990.
The field that students pursue does matter. Men who pursue business and women who pursue business and health can expect consistent and substantial returns.

Methodology to Assess Students' Post-College Earnings

Before the 1990s, a popular method for collecting information on former students was through survey instruments. Two major limitations of this method were the typically low response rate and the high cost of distributing a survey. Today, administrative databases have largely replaced the survey method.

In several states, the primary method for assessing the post-college earnings of students has been to use information maintained by the state's department of labor unemployment insurance (UI) wage record files. Employers are required to comply with the state's UI compensation law by submitting quarterly reports of the earnings of their employees. The collection and maintenance of this information is important for individuals who potentially are eligible to receive unemployment benefits. Further, should an individual become unemployed, the level of such benefits could be determined based on the information in the wage file. For each employee covered, an employer is required to report the employee's Social Security number (SSN) and the total amount of earnings received during the quarter. Additional information about the employer is also reported, such as the unique employer identification number, the county in which the business is reported, and the industrial affiliation of the business.

About twenty states have established a procedure to link higher education enrollment data with UI wage files (Seppanen, 1995). States that have employed this linking process include California, Florida, Illinois, Maryland, North Carolina, North Dakota, Oregon, South Carolina, Texas, and Washington. Some states, including Florida, Texas, and Washington, have developed a comprehensive system to account for students. Seppanen (1995) maintains that the issue of accountability, not research, was the motivating factor in developing a methodology to assess students' post-college earnings.

State Programs Using UI Wage Records. Questions about the contributions that community colleges make to an individual's economic worth have been quantified in terms of income enhancement. Several states have conducted statewide studies with wage record data to develop a methodology to assess students' post-college earnings. Most of the studies have followed program completers or graduates into the workplace to estimate average annual earnings or to determine placement. Collaborative efforts with the department of labor unemployment records offices have yielded information from the quarterly wage/earnings files for identified program completers or graduates. Since matching with the student's Social Security number is required to access not only earnings but also educational data, confidentiality and privacy issues have been a concern of researchers, policy makers, and state agencies. The following is a synopsis of state efforts in Florida, North Carolina, Texas, and Washington.

Florida. Florida is considered to be the pioneer in developing a follow-up strategy with UI wage record data. As a result of a legislative directive and a joint agreement between the state department of education and the department of labor and employment, the Florida Education and Training Placement Information Program (FETPIP) was developed (Pfeiffer, 1994). This data-linking procedure is by far the most comprehensive. To obtain follow-up data on employment, military service, and postsecondary education, the databases of state and federal agencies are collected (for example, departments of corrections, education, and defense, U.S. Postal Service). Currently, FETPIP provides follow-up services to over 75 programs and organizations on more than 1.8 million former students, participants, exconvicts, and trainees.

North Carolina. The Common Follow-up System (CFS) dates back to 1992, with seven agencies participating. In 1995 follow-up was required by law because the legislature was interested in examining the extent to which programs were doing their job. On the policy side of things, policy makers wanted to know whether these programs deserved funding. Currently, nine agencies are involved in the CFS. Efforts are under way to develop a common reporting procedure across agencies. The CFS is linked with the U.S. Postal Service, the Office of Personnel Management, the Department of Defense, and, most recently, the Department of Corrections. In 1993, adoption of a new legislation and goals statement for the North Carolina community college system reemphasized the efforts by community colleges on workforce preparedness (Vanderheyden, 1994). In response to this policy, efforts have been made to measure two outcomes of successful work force training: employment rates and median salary of program completers.

Texas. The state of Texas has been engaged in automated student follow-up for five years. Similar to most states, the UI wage records serve as the primary source of data to follow up students (Anderberg, 1994). Originally, the follow-up efforts were conducted by community colleges; however, the State Occupational Information Coordinating Committee (SOICC) has played an integral role in administering the data. An agency within the Texas state government and part of the federal network, the Texas SOICC performs many services, providing technical assistance on issues related to the labor market and occupational data. The primary purpose of SOICC is to collect, develop, and disseminate information on the labor market, including data on occupations, careers, and training. Like other states, Texas links the records on completers and leavers. State mandate further requires examination of students' occupations. For those who had specific occupational training, an employee survey is conducted to obtain the student's occupational title and the zip code of the worksite.

Washington. The Washington State Board for Community and Technical Colleges (WSBCTC) compiles data on educational and job-related outcomes for students leaving vocational preparation programs (Seppanen, 1993, 1994, 1995). Via an automated data-matching procedure, this method examines state unemployment insurance and benefit records, public postsecondary enrollments, U.S. armed forces enlistments, and state community college enrollments. Specifically, data are compiled on employment status, estimated annual wages, hours worked per week, the relation of employment to training, postsecondary or military status, and a host of other measures. To account for out-of-state employment of Washington program completers, efforts are made to collaborate with neighboring states such as Alaska, California, Idaho, and Oregon.

Accountability and Performance Measures

An accountability movement in higher education emerged in the 1980s (Ewell, 1994). The movement is attributed to fiscal restraints, the influence of the accreditation process, and state mandates. Prior to the emphasis on accountability, the assessment of student learning was a process involving the student and faculty, resulting in a measurement in the form of a grade (Astin, 1991; Banta, 1993; Boyer and Ewell, 1988; Ewell and Boyer, 1988). With more public access to information about the effectiveness and productivity of higher education institutions, accountability has become a buzzword among administrators, legislators, policy makers, and the general public.

Historically, concepts of accountability were based on a model of public higher education as a public utility. This concept was measured by the extent to which individuals were socially mobile and experienced a better quality of life as a consequence of their education. In the 1980s, *access* and *efficiency* were the terms associated with accountability, but times have since changed. Ewell (1994) maintains that a new kind of accountability has emerged because higher education is perceived as a "strategic investment" that should earn returns. Although the accountability measures of the 1980s have not vanished, new measures of student and institutional outcomes or outputs have emerged.

State-Mandated versus Federally Mandated Accountability. For community colleges, responding to accountability mandates has taken center stage.

In considering different types of accountability, it is important to distinguish between state-mandated and federally mandated accountability measures. An example of a state-mandated accountability measure is that passed by the California legislature in 1989 requiring community colleges to develop a statewide accountability program to address educational and fiscal performance (Outcalt and Rabin, 1998). Specifically, outcomes to be evaluated included student access, transfer programs and rates, student goal satisfaction, occupational preparation, and fiscal conditions of the college districts (MacDougall and Friedlander, 1990). Other states have similar accountability mandates.

At the federal level, the Carl D. Perkins Vocational and Applied Technology Education Act requires accountability for vocational-technical programs. Federal funds are made available to help provide vocational-technical education programs and services to youth and adults. These funds are awarded as grants to state education agencies. The awards to individual states are based on a formula of certain age groups and their per capita income. The Perkins Act defines vocational-technical programs as "organized educational programs offering sequences of courses directly related to preparing individuals for paid or unpaid employment in current or emerging occupations requiring other than a baccalaureate or advanced degree" (U.S. Department of Education, 1998).

As mandated by the Perkins Act, each state is required to develop core standards and measures of performance to evaluate the quality of its vocational-technical education programs. At a minimum, each state must include the following performance indicators (U.S. Department of Education, 1998):

Measures of learning and competency gains, including student progress in the achievement of basic and academic skills

One or more measures of performance such as competency attainment, job or work-skill attainment, retention in school, or placement in school, job, or military

Incentives and adjustments designed to encourage service to targeted groups and special population students

Procedures for expanding existing resources and methods used by other programs receiving federal assistance, such as the Job Training Partnership Act Program and the Job Opportunities and Basic Skills Training Program

Performance Measures.   According to a recent survey conducted by the State Higher Education Executive Officers (SHEEO, 1998), thirty-seven states reported using performance measures in some form. This number is more than double that of previous years. The survey also reported that twenty-three states used performance measures to inform consumers about higher education and to distribute state funds to higher education institutions. Some of the most commonly reported performance measures include graduation and transfer rates, faculty workload or productivity, follow-up satisfaction, and placement data on graduates. Regarding placement data on graduates, nineteen states reported having a performance measure in place.

SHEEO reported that twenty-three states are currently using performance measures in some form in the budgetary process. Eight states, including Tennessee, Colorado, Missouri, Arkansas, Ohio, Florida, Kentucky, and South Carolina, have a direct linkage, with funds allocated to institutional performance on goals and measures. Although it is still too early to ascertain the ultimate impact of performance-based funding, the true test to "determine the effectiveness of performance measures will be whether a positive change occurs in teaching and learning" (SHEEO, 1998, p. 3).

In 1994, the American Association of Community Colleges formed a Community College Roundtable (CCR) of educators who were asked to tackle the question: What are the core indicators of community college effectiveness? The primary objective of the CCR was to distill the many complex models, indicators, and methods of the effectiveness arena into a set of core indicators. These indicators reflect the functions of community colleges, external mandates, or constituency needs. To qualify as a core indicator, a measure must allow for generalizability across institutions, ease and efficiency of use, relevance to the community college mission, and significance of multiple customers (AACC 1994, p. 6).

According to the CCR report, effectiveness is made up of "three Ps": publics, performance, and perception (AACC, 1994). The report maintains that an effective community college must:

1. Engage in successful transactions with external factors (publics)
2. Be able to compare results achieved (performance) with needs and expectations
3. Provide information about performance in ways that build understanding (perception) of the college's mission and purpose (p. 8)

A total of thirteen core indicators were advanced. Some of the core indicators covered areas such as student achievement, transfer, persistence, performance, and citizenship. Core indicator 4 (Placement Rate in the Workforce) relates to the topic of this volume.

Placement rate in the workforce. The measure is the proportion of an identified cohort of entering community college students achieving a "marketable skill" (that is, completing at least three occupational-technical courses in particular fields of training) who obtain employment in a field directly related to this skill within one year of last attendance (AACC, 1994, pp. 18–19).

Data source(s). A follow-up questionnaire is administered to former students periodically by mail. If available, state employment information provides a more direct method of assessment. The obvious limitation of this methodology is that many state databases do not contain the required job information to identify occupation adequately. To date, only seven states possess this capability.

Additional measures. The following measures are recommended to better communicate effectiveness:

Reporting data for students according to prior credit earned at the community college and by whether a degree or certificate was earned

Reporting data for students according to occupation deemed both "directly and indirectly related" to the field of training

A statistic that reports the placement rate of all students enrolling for at least one occupational-technical course at the community college (this relaxes the "marketable skills" restriction contained in the core measure)

AACC's core indicator, which measures placement rate in the workforce, raises important questions. Since the indicator measures the extent to which community college students achieve a marketable skill and obtain employment in a field directly related to such skills, the assumption is made that students are working in fields they studied.

Conclusion

The accountability process calls for an evaluation of how colleges and their vocational programs are responding to external mandates, and whether they have internalized the importance of the performance information they generate in order to improve classroom instruction. It seems clear that some states and individual colleges have taken the lead in integrating post-college earnings into their program evaluation and operation.

For all the work that community colleges do in preparing students either to enter the world of work or to transfer to four-year institutions, they have not sufficiently studied the long-term effects on students in terms of post-college earnings. To some degree, it is this failure that has led to the onset of accountability mandates. With the wave of new state and federal legislation, community college advocates should continue working aggressively to develop measures and core indicators that better represent a variety of student outcomes.

References

Adams, W., and Jaffe, A. "Economic Returns on the College Investment." *Change*, 1971, *3*, 8.

American Association of Community Colleges. *Community Colleges: Core Indicators of Effectiveness.* Washington, D.C.: American Association of Community Colleges, 1994.

Anderberg, M. *Automated Student and Adult Learning Follow-Up System, Final Report for Program Year 1993–94.* Austin: Texas State Occupational Information Coordinating Committee, 1994.

Astin, A. W. *Achieving Educational Excellence.* San Francisco: Jossey-Bass, 1985.

Astin, A. W. *Assessment for Excellence: The Philosophy and Practice of Assessment and Evaluation in Higher Education.* New York: Macmillan, 1991.

Banta, T. W. *Making a Difference: Outcomes of a Decade of Assessment in Higher Education.* San Francisco, Calif.: Jossey-Bass, 1993.

Becker, G. S. *Human Capital: A Theoretical and Empirical Analysis, with Special Reference to Education.* (1st, 2nd, and 3rd eds.) New York: Columbia University Press, 1964, 1975, 1993.

Becker, G. S. "Why Go to College? The Value of an Investment in Higher Education." In W. E. Becker and D. R. Lewis (eds.), *The Economics of American Higher Education*. Boston: Kluwer Academic Publishers, 1992.

Boyer, C. M., and Ewell, P. T. *State-Based Approaches to Assessment in Undergraduate Education: A Glossary and Selected References*. Denver, Colo.: Education Commission of the United States, 1988.

Cohen, A. M., and Brawer, F. B. *American Community College*. San Francisco: Jossey-Bass, 1996.

Dougherty, K. J. *The Contradictory College: The Conflicting Origins, Impacts, and Futures of the Community College*. New York: State University of New York Press, 1994.

Eaton, J. *Colleges of Choice: The Enabling Impact of the Community College*. New York: Macmillan, 1994.

Ewell, P. T. "A Matter of Integrity: Accountability and the Future of Self-Regulation." *Change Magazine*, 1994, November/December, 25–29.

Ewell, P. T., and Boyer, C. M. "Acting Out State-Mandated Assessments: Evidence from Five States." *Change*, 1988, *20* (4): 40–47.

Grubb, W. N. *Working in the Middle: Strengthening Education and Training for the Mid-Skilled Labor Force*. San Francisco: Jossey Bass, 1996.

Haller, A. "Reflections on the Social Psychology of Status Attainment." In R. Hauser, D. Mechanic, A. Haller, and T. Hauser (eds.), *Social Structure and Behavior*. New York: Academic Press, 1982.

Henderson, C., and Ottinger, C. "College Degrees—Still a Ladder to Success?" *Journal of College Placement*, 1985, *45*, 33.

Jencks, C., Bartlett, S., Corcoran, M., Crouse, J., Eaglesfield, D., Jackson, G., McClelland, K. I., Mueser, P., Olneck, M., Schwarts, J., Ward, S., and William, J. *Who Gets Ahead? The Determinants of Economic Success in America*. New York: Basic Books, 1979.

Koltai, L. "Community Colleges: Making Winners Out of Ordinary People." In A. Levin (ed.), *Higher Learning in America: 1980–2000*. Baltimore: Johns Hopkins University Press, 1993.

MacDougall, P. R., and Friedlander, J. "A Proposed Accountability Model for California's Community Colleges: A Paper for Discussion." Santa Barbara, Calif.: Santa Barbara City College, 1990. (ED 314 123)

Outcalt, C., and Rabin, J. "Responding to Accountability Mandates." *ERIC Digest*. Los Angeles: ERIC Clearinghouse for Community Colleges, June 1998.

Pfeiffer, J. J. "Student Follow-up Using Automated Record Linkage Techniques: Lessons from Florida's Education and Training Placement Information Program (FETPIP)." *Journal of Vocational Education Research*, 1994, *19* (3), 83–105.

Romano, R. M. "What Is the Economic Payoff to a Community College Degree?" *Community/Junior College Quarterly of Research and Practice*, 1986, *10* (3), 153–164.

Sanchez, J. R., and Laanan, F. S. "Economic Benefits of Attending California Community Colleges." *Community College Review*, 1997, *25* (3), 73–87.

Seppanen, L. J. *Using Administrative Data Matches for Follow-Up*. Technical Report No. 93–5. Olympia: Washington State Board for Community and Technical Colleges, 1993. (ED 382 250)

Seppanen, L. J. *Job Placement for Graduates of Washington Community and Technical College Vocational Programs*. Research Report No. 94–7. Olympia: Washington State Board for Community and Technical Colleges, 1994. (ED 382 255)

Seppanen, L. J. "Linkages to the World of Employment." In P. T. Ewell (ed.), *Student Tracking: New Techniques, New Demands*. New Directions for Institutional Research, no. 87, 77–91. San Francisco: Jossey Bass, 1995.

State Higher Education Executive Officers (SHEEO). "Focus on Performance Measures." *Network News*, 1998, *17*, (1), February.

U.S. Department of Education. The Office of Vocational and Adult Education. [http://www.ed.gov/offices/OVAE/vocsite.html]. July 1998.

U.S. Department of Labor. *Occupational Outlook Quarterly,* Spring 1992, 40. Washington, D.C.: U.S. Department of Labor, Bureau of Labor Statistics.

Vanderheyden, B. *Employment of Community College Completers.* Research Brief No. 1994-01. Raleigh, N.C.: North Carolina State Department of Community Colleges, 1994. (ED 375 896)

JORGE R. SANCHEZ is director of vocational education and institutional research at Coast Community College District in Costa Mesa, California, and doctoral candidate in higher education at the University of California, Los Angeles.

FRANKIE SANTOS LAANAN is senior research analyst in vocational education and institutional research at Coast Community College District in Costa Mesa, California.

Across the country, vocational-technical centers, community colleges, and other postsecondary education entities are increasingly being held accountable by legislatures for student outcomes. In Florida, the accountability movement has spawned efforts to provide state funds based on outputs and outcomes, including earnings levels following graduation.

From Performance Reporting to Performance-Based Funding: Florida's Experiences in Workforce Development Performance Measurement

Jay J. Pfeiffer

On average, recipients of associate of science degrees from Florida's community colleges have been consistently shown to outearn most other postsecondary credential earners at all levels in their initial employment. On average, those earning bachelor's credentials do not approach the earnings of the associate of science recipients until five years after receiving their diplomas. Those earning postsecondary vocational certificates significantly outearn those without postsecondary credentials in their initial employment, and this difference in earnings persists over time. [These findings are documented in a succession of Annual Outcomes Reports generated by the Florida Education and Training Placement Information Program. Longitudinal comparisons of earnings are reported in *Apples and Oranges: Comparison of Outcomes for the Graduates of 1990–91* (Florida Department of Education, May 1997), and *Highways, Byways, and Sideways: Routes Taken by Florida's High School Graduates of 1990–91 Toward Baccalaureate Degrees* (Florida Department of Education, May 1998).]

The earnings levels are accompanied by high percentages of full-time, steady employment for former students that are typically related to the training that they received. Performance reports for community colleges and school districts have included measures of employment and earnings that reflect these types of outcomes for a long time. However, funding has been based primarily on full-time equivalency enrollment data—"seat time"—rather than on outcomes.

Even with funding decisions made on the basis of seat time, legislators, governors, business leaders, advisory groups, boards of trustees, and other groups have continually wanted to know the answers to questions such as, How many students completed their curriculum and graduated? How many students obtained employment as a result of the services they received? Are the jobs obtained by former students related to their training? How many participants are now off of the dole?

As a result of legislation in Florida, answers to these bottom-line types of questions will soon be the basis for the allocation of state revenue resources to postsecondary programs, including adult general and vocational education under the rubric of workforce development education. The ability of local institutions to earn state resources will be partially a function of the earning capacities of former students. This chapter traces the developments that have led to the establishment of a funding system based on student outputs and outcomes rather than on seat time.

Florida's Postsecondary Workforce Development System: Background

The primary components of Florida's workforce development system include elements of the secondary and postsecondary education system as well as job placement and job training operations. The postsecondary education components include twenty-eight community colleges and sixty of the state's sixty-seven school districts. Job placement and job training programs, primarily funded through the federal Job Training Partnership and Wagner Peyser Acts, are administered in twenty-four workforce development regions. The workforce development regions are used to organize services to welfare recipients through welfare reform initiatives.

Coordination among these components has proven difficult. Each is governed by different arrangements, regulations, and guidelines. Community colleges serve designated regional groupings of counties and are governed by a board of directors appointed by the governor. School districts serve countywide areas and are governed by elected school boards. Workforce development regions serve multicounty regions and are overseen by locally appointed, governor-sanctioned, workforce development boards. Welfare reform initiatives are delivered through governing coalitions—boards appointed by the governor to oversee operations in regions that are contiguous with the workforce development regions. Some of the coalitions are organized as a part of the workforce development boards. Some are separate entities that maintain a cooperative relationship with the boards. A significant aspect of improving coordination has focused on developing performance measurement tools and requirements.

Putting the Pieces in Place: Initial Performance Requirements and Measurement Tools. Until 1984, success in Florida's workforce development system, particularly in postsecondary vocational and adult education, was gauged largely through anecdotal information. Although systematic follow-up data were gathered through standardized postcard surveys, data were not used for the regular evaluation of programs. Funding for programs was based on student seat time determined by periodic student surveys conducted locally and reported to the state level in aggregate form.

In 1984, the Florida legislature established a placement performance requirement for vocational programs. The requirement was that in order to assure continued funding, programs had to demonstrate annually and sustain a 70 percent training-related placement rate. *Training-related* meant employment in related occupations, continued postsecondary education, and/or service in the military. Though funding continued to be based on student seat time, this initiative added a requirement for continued funding based on program outcome. At the same time, the legislature moved to provide funding for measurement tools in the form of data management systems. One effort was to fund the development of statewide student information systems for school districts and community colleges at a unit-record level. Another effort was to establish the Florida Education and Training Placement Information Program (FETPIP).

Florida's Education and Training Placement Information Program. FETPIP is an interagency data collection system that obtains follow-up data on former students. The former students include all public school system high school graduates and dropouts, all community college associate degree and vocational students, all secondary and postsecondary vocational students, all state university system graduates, adult education and General Educational Development (GED) students, selected private vocational school graduates, state college and university graduates, all Job Training Partnership Act program participants, welfare reform participants, unemployment insurance claimants, and correctional system releases. Organizations representing each group provide FETPIP with individual student or participant files from their management information system units. The files include individual identifiers (name, social security number) as well as demographic, socioeconomic, and programmatic data.

FETPIP collects follow-up data that describe employment, military enlistment, incarceration, public assistance participation, and continuing education experiences. It electronically links participants' files to the administrative records of eight states and federal agencies. In addition, FETPIP annually contacts about 25,000 employers to determine the occupations and county locations of students that were found in their employ. These data are combined with earnings data to assist analysts at the local level in relating employment experiences to education or training experiences.

FETPIP emerged as the primary means of measuring and reporting a variety of outcomes for the state's workforce development programs. Its evolution set the stage to develop common performance measures that could be applied across all elements of the workforce development system. This capability led to several efforts to consolidate performance measures for workforce development.

Consensus Measures: Consolidating Vocational Education Performance Measures. Section 115 of the federal Carl D. Perkins Act requires that states appoint *committees of practitioners* to assist in the development and implementation of a statewide system of core performance standards and measures. This system addresses measures of learning and competency gains as well as measures of performance, and includes incentives that encourage the provision of services to targeted populations. Through the work of its practitioners committee in 1992, Florida adopted a system that included ten measures. Because a wide audience of education and training professionals were directly involved in developing these measures, they are referred to as *consensus measures*. Subsequently, the legislature modified the training-related placement requirement to adopt these consensus measures. Each measure depends on data from the student-level databases maintained in Tallahassee as well as outcome information from the FETPIP system. The idea behind developing the system of measures was to report performances to the federal level, as was required by the Perkins Act, and to provide performance information for state and local management.

The system includes one process-type measure, an enrollment rate for targeted populations. It also includes output measures such as completion and leaver rates and student gains in basic and academic skills. There are five outcome measures, including completer and leaver job placement rates, a comparison of these rates to all terminators, and earning levels for students at the specific program level as well as at the institution level. Each measure includes separate calculations for targeted populations, such as disabled and disadvantaged students.

Additional Performance Requirements. The federal Job Training Partnership Act and federal/state welfare reform initiatives contain performance measurement requirements. These had to be considered when public postsecondary education was used as a strategy to improve the employability of clients targeted by these initiatives.

The Job Training Partnership Act. Section 106 of the federal Job Training Partnership Act requires that the secretary of the U.S. Department of Labor establish performance standards for various programs under the act. These standards may be revised every two years. Changes are promulgated through official guidance letters. The latest guidance letter, number 4–95 dated May 3, 1996, outlines current performance goals and standards. The goals include improving the quality and intensity of services to disadvantaged adults to improve their long-term employability and earnings; raising the quality of placements to include above-poverty wages, full-time work, and benefits; helping youth attain skill enhancements leading to employment or continuing education; and improving the employment prospects of laid-off workers for jobs that pay equal to, or better than, the jobs they left.

Measures of these goals are also promulgated through the guidance letters. Specific measures include adult, youth, welfare recipient, laid-off worker, and older worker employment rates; adult, welfare recipient, and older worker earnings; and youth employability enhancement rates.

The state of Florida recently adopted a waiver plan, approved by the U.S. Department of Labor, which allows the state to collect performance measurement data by means other than those mandated by the Secretary of Labor. Alternative collection strategies require some adjustment in the measures themselves. This will improve the compatibility of the standards to other workforce programs in the state, including FETPIP.

Florida's Welfare Reform Initiative: Work and Gain Economic Self-Sufficiency (WAGES). When the WAGES bill was passed by the 1996 legislature, it included a provision for the development of outcome measures that would, to the degree possible, be consistent with measures adopted in support of the Workforce Florida Act. In response, nine outcome-related performance measures are proposed in conjunction with welfare-to-work initiatives. They include program and approved employment participation rates for participants, a job placement rate after participation, several earnings measures after participation, and an employment retention measure. There are also several measures dealing with enrollment in and duration of enrollment in vocational education and supported work experience.

Consolidating Measures: The Workforce Florida Act

In its 1996 session, the Florida legislature passed the Workforce Florida Act to foster a unified workforce development system. Among other stipulations, the law calls for the consolidation of various performance measurement approaches into a single system. The single system is to be structured into three measurement tiers. With state level unit record data on students and participants in workforce development programs and the FETPIP system, legislators felt that they had the tools necessary to establish a system of common measures that could be applied broadly across the entire workforce development system at the state level (the first tier), more detailed program initiatives (meaning broad workforce initiatives such as welfare reform, school-to-work, postsecondary education focusing on high skills, and job placement) at the state and regional level (the second tier), and very detailed operations at the local level (the third tier, which deals with day-to-day management of programs that combine core measures with additional data and measures to facilitate operations).

Tier 1 measures are to be applied against all workforce education and development programs for system-wide performance measurement.

1. Initial entered employment rate level I. This is expressed as a number and percentage of those who completed/terminated workforce development activities and who obtained employment at an earnings level equal to or above the minimum wage at the equivalent of full-time/full-quarter employment.
2. Initial entered employment rate level II. This is the number and percentage of those who obtained employment at or above the lower level entry

wage established through the Occupational Forecasting Conference (OFC). Established by the Workforce Florida Act, OFC is charged with identifying high-skill, high-wage job opportunities to be targeted by education, training, and economic development programs in the state.

3. Initial entered employment rate level III. This is the number and percentage of those who obtained employment at or above the level II threshold and who were employed in high wage/high skill occupations defined by the Occupational Forecasting Conference.

4. Continued employment. This measure is based on three years of continuous follow-up. Its purpose is to examine retention in employment.

5. Public assistance dependence. This is the number and rate of those receiving cash payments (Aid to Families with Dependent Children/Temporary Aid for Needy Families) and/or food stamps after program completion/termination.

6. Continued dependence on public assistance. This is measured based on three years of continuous follow up. It represents a measure of continued dependence after program participation.

7. Return on investment. This is measured based on implementation of a cost consequences analysis methodology. The current methodology compares the amount of funds invested in specific job preparation programs to the resulting self-sufficiency of program participants measured in terms of postprogram earnings, reduced reliance on public assistance benefits, and increased payroll revenues.

8. Continued education. This measure consists of the number and rate of program participants/students who pursued further postsecondary education.

Tier 2 measures are to be used at the workforce development program component level. For example, postsecondary vocational education would be one component. *All Tier 1 measures would also be expressed at this level as Tier 2 measures.*

1. Entered employment rate. The rate at which completers/terminees obtain any employment.

2. Earnings at entered employment. The average earnings for all of those found in measure 1.

3. Earnings growth. This is calculated based on those who were retained in employment.

4. Cost per entered employment. This is calculated based on data contained in the cost consequences model referred to above.

Tier 3 measurements include those mandated by specific state or federal laws and those necessary for ongoing management and performance diagnostics. The third tier would be applied at very specific program levels. *All Tier 1 and Tier 2 measures would be expressed as Tier 3 measures.* The measures include agency initiatives or program-specific output and outcome measures necessary to meet reporting requirements (state or federal) and day-to-day program management requirements.

Consolidating Measures: The U.S. Department of Labor's Workforce Development Performance Measures Initiative

In 1997, the U.S. Department of Labor brought together federal, state, and local representatives from Job Training Partnership Act–type workforce development operations, vocational education programs, vocational rehabilitation services, adult general education programs, and other workforce development interests. Their purpose was to develop a set of common performance measures with standard definitions that could be applied across all elements of the national workforce development system. The group met several times for over a year to come up with eight core key indicators of success. The measures include an initial employment rate, employment retention, earnings gains, improved self-sufficiency, skills attainment, continued education rates, and customer satisfaction indicators.

The system of core measures that were posed became the basis for measures that will soon be required for programs funded through H.R. 1385, the Workforce Investment Act of 1998.

Florida's Move to Performance-Based Funding

In addition to establishing performance measurement tiers and working toward a more unified workforce development system, the Workforce Florida Act inaugurated a pilot experiment in performance-based funding, referred to as *Performance-Based Incentive Funding* (PBIF).

Performance-Based Incentive Funding. With PBIF, local community college and school district administrators can receive additional funds as incentives for certain postsecondary vocational programs. The certain vocational programs are restricted to those determined through the Occupational Forecasting Conference as leading to high-skill, high-wage, high-demand occupations.

PBIF establishes an incentive pot of money composed of funds from the Job Training Partnership Act and welfare reform initiatives as well as some state funds. Participating institutions provide a matching amount to the incentive pot based on previous performances for the high-skill, high-wage vocational programs. The performances are all based on output and outcome information, with the exception of an enrollment incentive for economically disadvantaged students. Extra weights are applied to the outputs (completions) and outcomes (placements) when the students are economically disadvantaged, disabled, or persons whose primary language is not English and whose skills in English are limited. The enrollments and completions are documented through student databases whereas placements are documented through quarterly FETPIP runs.

Performance-Based Program Budgeting: (PB)2. Though this chapter focuses on workforce development, note that sectors of government operations are not immune to performance-based budgeting issues. The Florida legislature called for increased levels of budgeting based on outcomes and outputs in all government sectors. Ultimately they established the Performance-Based Program Budgeting process, known as (PB)2, for all state agencies.

(PB)2 is designed to address issues of accountability and budgeting. Essentially, budgets should be developed based on the same types of performance requirements that are expected of public agencies by the public. By developing budgets around these expectations, the budgeting process should become more understandable to the general public. On a phase-in schedule developed through the governor's office, state agencies are to propose (PB)2 measures, have them jointly approved by the governor and legislature, and thereafter use them in the preparation of annual budgets. Each agency is required to establish a clear vision, identify key public/stakeholder expectations, and propose solutions. Annual budget proposals are to be structured around inputs, processes, outputs, and outcomes categories.

Inputs chart the operating environment and resources. Such data might include populations to be served, economic conditions, previous budgets, and revenue sources. *Processes* describe operations, organizational structures, and costs. *Outputs* describe the quantity and quality of services. *Outcomes* are the accomplishments, that is, the results. The expected outcomes in any given year become part of the inputs for subsequent budget cycles.

The Full Move: S.B. 1688 Workforce Education Program Fund

In its 1997 session, Florida's legislature passed an initiative that put all state funding—over $731 million—for adult general and postsecondary vocational education into a single unified program fund. The initiative is known as S.B. 1688. Previously, these dollars were divided into several categories under two primary program funds. One of these was for community colleges, the Florida Community College Program Fund. The other was part of a broad funding program that included K–12 education, the Florida Education Finance Program. Whereas local institutions qualified for dollars under these programs based on full-time-equivalent enrollments, the new program made this allocation on the basis of specified performances.

The original funding formula, which was included in the law as it was passed in 1997, had a complicated funding formula based on cumulative student enrollment hours, program completions, various types of job placement, and the cost of instructional programs. There was a great deal of concern at the state and local levels that the existing student databases and the FETPIP system would not be able to support the data needs of the proposed formula.

Because of these concerns, the 1998 legislature introduced changes to the law, including the funding formula.

An initial review of the new version of the law, which is to be implemented in the next budget cycle, suggests a funding formula that can be seen as having six steps. It is anchored on a one-time appropriation to each school district with postsecondary programs and each community college for the 1998–1999 fiscal year. The one-time appropriation provides each college and district with the state funds needed to operate adult general and postsecondary education programs. The one-time amount to each local area will serve as the base amount for the first year of a performance formula–driven process. The budgeting for this process will begin in December 1998.

Key Terms. The law defines six major categories of programs to be considered in funding. These include continuing workforce education, vocational certificate, apprenticeship, applied technology diploma, associate of science degree, and adult general education programs. S.B. 1688 requires statewide consistency in the curricula and length of programs in each of these categories.

The law defines two general types of performances to be paid for. These include performance output measures and performance outcome measures. *Performance output measures* deal with program completion. For vocational programs, completions are measured at occupational completion points. These are potential exit points for each vocational program where students can obtain training-related employment. They are somewhat analogous to leavers with marketable skills. For adult general education programs, completions are measured at literacy completion points, that is, exit points that reflect substantial student improvement in one of the aspects of the competencies that are taught in adult general education. Other completion points might reflect the attainment of a state high school diploma via the GED test or an adult high school diploma. *Performance outcome measures* deal with post-program placement measured through the FETPIP program.

There are four levels of placement that will be the basis of outcome payouts. Level I is for a placement in any job or continuing postsecondary education enrollment at a higher level. Level II is for job placements that fall within the $7.50 to $9.00 per hour range in high-skill occupations designated by the Occupational Forecasting Conference. Included in level II is continuing postsecondary enrollments in associate-degree or university-level programs. Level III is for placements in jobs that pay above $9.00 per hour. Level IV deals with employment retention a year after initial employment. The retention measure may include a provision that will only apply if the employment is at a higher earnings level than the initial employment.

The Funding Formula. The funding formula is generally prescribed in the legislation. It is expected that it will be refined each year as new data and priorities emerge. The formula is to be applied on an annual basis with the most recently available data. For the 1999–2000 fiscal year, the formula will be based on the most recent full year of enrollment and completion data (1997–1998). It will include the most recent annual FETPIP follow-up data (based on

1996–1997 completers with 1995–1996 retention information). Data reported for 1998–1999 will be considered to account for trends in enrollment and completion. The formula will be formally run in December in advance of the next legislative session. At the time of this writing, the exact formula had not been finalized. Finalization will include the exact specification of the formula, including the assignment of weighting values for different levels of completion and placement. Based on provisions of the legislation and several simulation efforts, the formula may be expected to work as follows:

Step 1. Divide the total appropriation into five component parts. The total appropriation for the Workforce Development Education Program Fund is more than $731 million (the exact amount is $731,581,719; in addition, the legislature provided a $16,500,000 capitalization grant amount to assist local institutions in initiating new programs). For this discussion, this will be treated as the total funding that is available. The component parts are those categories that are to be treated differently in calculating unit performance values. For purposes of this step, the six legislated categories were reduced to five by combining the applied technology diploma programs with the associate of science programs. The five categories are continuing workforce education, vocational certificate, apprenticeship, applied technology diploma and associate of science degree, and adult general education. The five categories are derived by using the statewide full-time-equivalent enrollment values from the most recently available annual data.

Step 2. Subdivide each category. Fifteen percent of each category will be calculated. The fifteen percent amount will be used to calculate unit values for completions and placements.

Step 3. Calculate performance unit values. Statewide aggregated completions and placements are divided into the same five funding categories. For example, this means that all of the completions for vocational certificates will be added up for the target year, as will all of the placements. These will be added using weighting values that will be assigned. Completions from longer programs will be weighted more than completions from short programs. Placements at high-earning levels and for retention will be weighted more heavily than placements in low-earning jobs. Similarly, weights will be assigned based on certain hard-to-serve individual characteristics such as certain types of disabilities and economic disadvantage. The total weighted completions and the total weighted placements will be divided into the 15 percent share. This will produce a dollar value for each weighted performance.

Step 4. Calculate base local appropriations. Each community college and school district with postsecondary programs will receive 85 percent of its prior year's funding as a base amount. This is the starting place for calculating a total appropriation.

Step 5. Calculate performance awards. For each community college and school district, the different types of completion and placement will be totaled. Each total will be multiplied times the unit values calculated in step 3. This total performance value will be added to the base amount calculated in step 4.

Step 6. Adjust for economically depressed areas. The legislation provides that adjustments be made to provide extra rewards to school districts and community colleges that successfully place students in the midst of periods of high unemployment.

Readers will note that the general scheme of the funding formula is that an 85 percent local base amount is augmented with performance awards originally calculated on the basis of 15 percent of the statewide total appropriation. Simply put, local entities can earn a larger amount than they were provided in the previous year if they have large numbers of completions and placements. This is particularly true if the completions are from longer-length programs and the placements are in high-wage jobs. It is also particularly true if the placements include large numbers of hard-to-serve individuals. If, however, completions and placements are not forthcoming, the local entity will receive less than its previous year's appropriation. The difficulty then is that the appropriation serves as the basis for the 85 percent base amount in the next cycle.

There is much work to do during the 1998–1999 fiscal year to put in place the mechanisms that are necessary to implement this law. Chief among them is upgrading the information infrastructure for the community college and school district systems. This includes developing new reporting sequences and new and revised data elements and, in many instances, significantly improving the accuracy of what is reported. This latter point is critical. Many of the data elements reported in the past were relatively low-stakes data elements, meaning that funding was not contingent on their accuracy. The new funding program will require a rapid move to improve the accuracy of these elements.

Conclusion

This chapter has traced efforts in Florida to respond to the questions typically asked of legislators, governors, education commissioners, and other policy makers, noted at the beginning—How many students completed their curriculum and graduated? How many students obtained employment as a result of the services they received? Are the jobs obtained by former students related to their training? How many participants are now off of the dole? Responses of this sort are generally categorical—they are designed to apply to a limited set or type of education or training programs. In Florida, the efforts can be characterized as moving toward comprehensive application, that is, toward development of common information tools and the emergence of core performance expectations.

The essential character of the performance-based funding approach being pursued in Florida is to put emphasis on outputs and outcomes. The measures associated with completions are intended to add value to finishing programs. Redefining completions as occupational and literacy completion points is intended to provide for exit points associated with education and workforce competencies where a departing student can obtain employment or pursue a further education goal. A completion measure by itself, however, could influence a proliferation of very short programs without important outcomes.

The measures associated with placements (and continuing education) and increasing value on higher wage placements and job retention are intended to assure that completion points represent valid exit points. The higher value placed on higher earnings should influence the degree to which programs focus on high-skill, high-wage, and high-demand jobs. Generally, this means longer programs. Although the emphasis on completion and placement is important, it could preclude the enrollment of students who need more time and attention to succeed. The proposed formula attempts to underscore the necessity of providing education services to hard-to-serve students by including weights—extra points—for these students when they complete and obtain employment.

Combinations of measures that will influence and balance the demands for high completion/graduation rates, high-level outcomes, and services to all types of students are essential characteristics of a sound performance-based funding approach. As the system in Florida matures, it will be important to hone the approach to assure that the workforce development system performs as it is intended. One consideration will be the incorporation of factors that will provide extra incentives for the creation of employment and education opportunities where they are sparsely available. Another will be to influence how various programs are combined to deal with the employability needs of students who have education and experience deficits that preclude successful participation in the labor market.

JAY J. PFEIFFER is education policy director of the Workforce Education and Outcome Information Services Unit of the Florida Department of Education. He has dealt with performance measurement and follow-up statistics and their applications in state workforce development policy in Florida for over twenty years.

The author shares insights from a decade of experience using administrative records, primarily the unemployment insurance wage records, to learn about the outcomes of job preparatory training in the community and technical colleges in Washington State.

Translating Data into Useful Information and Knowledge

Loretta Seppanen

Since the late 1980s the Washington State Board for Community and Technical Colleges (SBCTC) has linked college data files with other administrative records to provide outcomes data on the earnings and employment status of former students. The data sources include the unemployment insurance system in the state of Washington and neighboring states and higher education enrollment records. The process of translating data into information and new knowledge begins with tackling the issues inherent in the use of databases not designed for outcomes analysis (Seppanen, 1995). These data must be translated into meaningful, useful information (databases, reports, and presentations). Finally, as this information leads to new conversations about the relationship between education and labor market outcomes, it can bring about new common understanding, that is, new knowledge.

This chapter provides a summary of the new knowledge resulting from the use of these administrative records in Washington State. It also includes information that is only now becoming part of our conversations. The reader is invited to participate in the process of creating new knowledge. The chapter concludes with a summary of the choices Washington State has made regarding translating data into information, particularly related to the use of the unemployment insurance wage (UI) files.

Washington Community and Technical Colleges

The thirty-two community and technical colleges are largely state-funded institutions with no local tax base. Each institution receives funding from the Washington State legislature as a portion of the allocation to the SBCTC located in the state capital, Olympia. Each year the thirty-two colleges serve 400,000 students. The colleges graduate 12,000 job-oriented students from degree and certificate programs. Colleges also send another 12,000 students without degrees and certificates directly to the workforce from those same programs.

The typical job-oriented student is thirty-one years of age. The majority of job-oriented students are women; 22 percent are students of color. The single largest job-oriented program, in terms of number of graduates, is the secretarial and administrative support area with 1,060 graduates, followed by the associate degree nursing program with 890 graduates in the most recent year.

The data linking described here is limited to the 24,000 students leaving the colleges after preparing for new jobs. It does not include transfer students or students enrolled for a few classes to upgrade skills.

Partnership Effort

Since 1987, the SBCTC has linked the records of former students from all thirty-two colleges with those of the state's Employment Security Department (ESD). A few years later the managers of the Job Training Partnership Act (JTPA), high schools, and other workforce programs also began separate efforts to link participant records with ESD files. Maintaining the separate processes proved increasingly expensive for each agency. The separate processes also resulted in different approaches to reporting placement rates and earnings. In 1997, under the leadership of the state's workforce policy board, the Workforce Training and Education Coordinating Board (WTECB), these groups joined forces to develop a common, yet decentralized, and less costly approach to data linking.

DLOA Steps. The partnership provides the SBCTC and indirectly the colleges with a product called Data Linking for Outcomes Assessment (DLOA). The DLOA is created in several steps. The first involves the linking of college files with the UI file and university records. The result is a huge file that is extremely difficult to use, with hundreds of records for each student. Essentially it contains one record for every three-month period during the past six years. For each period there is a record for every firm for which the student worked and for every college the student attended.

The second step involves combining, sorting, and labeling that huge file. During the second step, computer protocols translate data from these many records into a format that meets the requirements of the common data standards and is easy to use. At this time, the DLOA is stored as an Access 7.0 database, a commonly used microcomputer software product.

The K–12 system, the Employment Security Department, the WTECB, and SBCTC share the cost of these first two steps. Employment Security staff does the work of the first step. A software-engineering firm working under contract for the combined agencies does the second step. SBCTC typically links about 200,000 student records a year at a cost of about $.07 per record.

SBCTC staff is responsible for the third step. The staff adds student course-taking and demographic information to this already rich database, and separates the statewide database into separate files for each college. Finally, college staffs use their DLOA to find the answers to a wide-ranging set of questions of interest.

DLOA Contents. The DLOA contains extensive data for each former student. Fortunately, modern computer software allows fast access to this rich data. For each student, the DLOA has up to eighteen records describing employment and college attendance in the four years before enrollment in the vocational program, a similar number of records describing employment while in college, and fourteen records describing employment and continuing education after the student's leaving the two-year system. For each student these records include the total quarterly earnings; the industry of the main employer, reported using the Department of Labor's Standard Industry Code; and the county where that employer is located.

This information is not unique to Washington State. It is available in all UI systems. What is unique to Washington is the availability of hours worked in the quarter. Washington has collected hours-worked data for more than a decade to meets its needs related to unemployment insurance claims. A claimant must meet a threshold of 600 hours worked to be eligible for unemployment insurance. Based on this information, our DLOA includes a calculated hourly wage rate.

Much of our analysis is based on this hourly wage data, as can be seen in the data tables in this chapter. Although similar information is not currently available in most other states, researchers can substitute monthly earnings (quarterly earnings divided by three). Researcher David Stevens (1996) has provided numerous examples of the value of the quarterly earnings data for outcomes assessment.

Ease of Use. Although the DLOA data are extensive, the typical researcher can find what is needed quickly. A simple query provides the information shown in Table 3.1 for all graduates of a program in the third quarter after college. By making a change in just one data element in the query, the researcher can look at the same students a year later, or in the third quarter before college, or while they were enrolled. This quick access is a DLOA design feature based on indexing employment relative to the time when a student began and ended college.

Table 3.1 provides actual data for each library assistant program graduate six to nine months after college. The table shows the hourly wage along with the industry of employment. This table could also easily include the county of employment. Clearly most of the library assistant graduates are working in industries that match well with their training. Half earned $9.50 an hour or more, a wage consistent with the student educational investment.

Table 3.1. Library Assistant Graduates' Employment Status, Six to Nine Months After College (Class of 1995–96)

Student	1997 Rate	Industry
1	$15.05	Hospitals
2	$12.48	Libraries and information centers
3	$11.87	Libraries and information centers
4	$11.71	Colleges and universities
5	$10.84	Miscellaneous amusement, recreational services
6	$10.42	Mutual savings banks
7	$10.38	Computer and data processing services
8	$10.12	Legal services
9	$10.06	Colleges and universities
10	$9.60	Elementary and secondary schools
11	$9.25	Libraries and information centers
12	$8.50	Elementary and secondary schools
13	$8.33	Colleges and universities
14	$7.96	Libraries and information centers
15	$7.67	Toys and sporting goods
16	$7.47	Research, development services
17	$7.11	Personnel supply services (temps)
18	$6.00	Miscellaneous business services
19	$5.99	Individual and family services
20	$5.94	Elementary and secondary schools

Before DLOA, SBCTC used a system that provided considerably fewer data in a less user-friendly format. Nevertheless, it provided sufficient useful information to serve as the basis for the creation of new knowledge.

Transforming Data into Useful Information

In addition to providing colleges with a database for their own use, SBCTC use these data in publications and reports to the state board, legislative committees, and college staff. As policy makers and college staff review these findings, new understandings emerge about the relationship between training and labor market outcomes, thus converting the data to information and then into new knowledge.

Examples of the information from the DLOA include an ongoing series of reports describing the outcomes of retraining workers laid off from their jobs as a result of structural changes in the economy; these represent the most extensive use of UI data, especially wage data (SBCTC, 1995). These accountability reports for the specially funded Worker Retraining Program are available in the publication sections of the SBCTC Web site: http://www.SBCTC.ctc.edu. Placement and earnings data for all students are published in the annual Academic Year Report, also available on-line (Student Progress and Success section of the annual report).

Transforming Information into New Knowledge

Over the years the information from the data-linking effort has led to three conclusions: (1) that our placement rates mirror national averages, (2) that it pays for students to graduate from two-year college programs, and (3) that not all programs benefit students equally. These conclusions are not unique to Washington community and technical colleges. Still, it has been important that we have access to our own data to confirm their applicability to the students in this state.

Placement Rates Mirror National Averages. In Washington, as in many states, placement rates were the main impetus for using administrative records. Year after year our DLOA-based employment rate for graduates has remained at about 83 percent, mirroring the national data for adults with two-year degrees. This rate has held close to constant through the fairly major ups and downs of the business cycles in Washington State.

As I have described elsewhere (Seppanen, 1995), administrative records do not currently provide a direct source for calculation of an employment rate. The DLOA provides a rate for those employed in jobs covered by the unemployment insurance system in Washington and several neighboring states and in federal employment. This "in covered employment rate" is meaningful from a research perspective but is difficult to use for public accountability purposes. Our rate for graduates of Washington community and technical colleges is 70 percent, a rate that is much lower than the public might expect from its two-year colleges. The employment of entrepreneurs and those working outside the Pacific Northwest is missing from the "in covered employment rate." SBCTC estimates this missing factor using results from periodic surveys of former students missing from the linked records (repeated every five years). Based on the most recent survey, we estimate that an additional nine percent of graduates are self-employed and four percent are employed outside our region. Thus, using the DLOA 70 percent in covered employment rate and the estimates from the survey, we put our overall estimated employment of graduates at 83 percent. We have used the same approach to estimate the employment of those who leave without a degree or certificate at 76 percent.

At a national level the Current Population Survey (CPS) provides the comparison employment rate for all adults with a two-year degree at 83 percent. The data in Figure 3.1 shows the typical pattern for the United States by educational level of workers for a single week during a year. The DLOA data provide employment rates for a quarter during a year.

It Pays to Graduate. As just discussed, graduates (degree and certificate combined) are employed at a higher rate than nongraduates. The DLOA also provides evidence that graduates earn more than those who did not receive a certificate or degree but have completed some units (called *leavers* in Table 3.2). Table 3.2 shows the recent earnings trend. The graduate wage advantage is declining somewhat as the economy in Washington improves. The data for the 1995–1996 class reflecting employment in late 1996 to early 1997 shows

Figure 3.1. Employment-to-Population Ratio by Educational Attainment for Adults 25 to 64 Years of Age, 1996

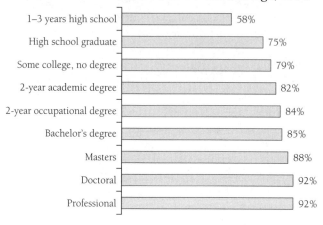

1–3 years high school	58%
High school graduate	75%
Some college, no degree	79%
2-year academic degree	82%
2-year occupational degree	84%
Bachelor's degree	85%
Masters	88%
Doctoral	92%
Professional	92%

Source: Mortenson, 1997, based on U.S. Current Population Survey. Used with permission.

Table 3.2. Inflation-Adjusted Hourly Wages for Job Preparatory Students (in 1997 Dollars)

	Class of 1993–1994	Class of 1994–1995	Class of 1995–1996
Graduates	$10.28	$10.44	$10.65
Leavers	$8.81	$8.80	$9.72
All	$9.59	$9.70	$10.17
Leaver wage as a percentage of graduate wage	86 %	84 %	91 %

less than a $1 an hour difference between graduates and leavers. Three years earlier, when the economy was just coming out of a slump, graduates earned about $1.50 more than students without a credential.

The literature on returns to college supports our conclusion about the benefit of completing training (Grubb, 1995). Some of the literature more precisely concludes that the more credits a student takes the more positive the earnings outcomes, irrespective of the credential (Kane and Rouse, 1993). Despite this literature, the view that completing a vocational degree or certificate pays has not always been part of the common belief in Washington community and technical colleges. A more common view was that job preparatory students who left a program prior to graduation did so in response to excellent employment opportunities. The substantial numbers of students who left college early for a wide variety of other reasons whose earning might not be so high went unnoticed. Each year about a third of those leaving job preparation are graduates. About a third leave almost immediately, completing less than 10 quarter credits in any vocational courses. Another third complete some units beyond the 10 credits but do not obtain a degree or certificate. The leaver data reported in this chapter apply to this group with 10 or more credits.

In addition to earning more after college than those who leave early, graduates from high-demand, high-wage programs also have greater wage gains. Before they started college, eventual graduates from the programs that typically draw high wages made $10.22 an hour (in 1997 dollars). At six to nine months after college they earned $13.70 an hour (also in 1997 dollars). The nongraduates in the same occupations, each taking about a year of course work, went from a precollege wage of $11.20 to $12.50 after college, a 12 percent increase compared to the 34 percent increase for graduates. Research shows that most of that 34 percent inflation-adjusted increase is due to the additional credits completed (WTECB, 1997; Westat, 1997).

This new knowledge that completing more college credits pays has made retention efforts a high priority. Colleges are looking for ways to improve the rate at which students continue at college until they achieve their goal. Colleges have implemented new introduction-to-college classes, more opportunities for career advising and goal clarification, and strategies to increase students' involvement in their learning.

Not All Programs Have Equal Benefits. In using data from the longitudinal Survey of Income and Program Participant data, Grubb (1995) showed that some programs of study appeared to provide no gain for students. In Washington, we have come to the common understanding that what students earn depends a good deal on their program of study. The wages for each program of study may be related to labor market factors rather than program quality. We have not yet formed a common view that the programs with lower earnings are a sign of no gain for the students, though there is some evidence to that effect (Westat, 1997).

Given the importance of program difference in potential earnings, we have begun to publish rank order listings of programs based on the typical wages of graduates as shown in Table 3.3. This rank may be related to labor market factors as well as program quality. In the highest-ranking programs the typical graduate earns $11 an hour or more. In the lowest-ranking programs the typical graduate earns between $7 and $9 an hour. For programs with at least 100 students statewide, these rankings are stable over time. Variation does occur with program changes, however. For example, the protective services program was historically near the bottom of the middle group but is now at the top. Many colleges have updated the correctional programs to provide the specific skills needed in the growing state prison systems.

Table 3.3. Washington Community and Technical Colleges 1995–96 Graduates and Leavers by Hourly Wages Six to Nine Months After College

| | Graduates | | Leavers | | |
Area of Training	Number	1997 $ Median	Number	1997 $ Median	Difference*
Associate degree nurse	886	$15.93	169	$10.69	$5.24
Practical nurse	340	$12.27	106	$9.21	$3.06
Information tech	489	$12.05	849	$11.68	$0.37
Electronics tech	219	$11.68	220	$11.49	$0.19
Electrical equipment repair	239	$11.36	148	$10.90	$0.46
All High Wage Areas Combined	2,173	$13.62	1,492	$11.53	$2.09
Protective services	351	$10.81	650	$10.11	$0.70
Legal assistant	268	$10.53	294	$11.38	–$0.85
Dental assisting	242	$10.38	50	$7.47	$2.91
Auto diesel	435	$10.26	648	$9.23	$1.03
Managerial and managerial support	380	$10.03	657	$10.19	–$0.16
Accounting	436	$9.15	493	$10.05	–$0.90
All Middle Wage Areas Combined	2,112	$10.07	2,792	$9.83	$0.24
Administrative support (secretarial)	1,060	$8.63	1,273	$8.36	$0.27
Marketing and sales	434	$8.27	447	$8.78	–$0.51
Nursing assistant	201	$7.92	73	$8.41	–$0.49
Early childhood education	260	$7.71	425	$8.13	–$0.42
Cosmetology	268	$7.29	158	$7.43	–$0.14
All Low Wage Areas Combined	2,223	$8.43	2,376	$8.39	$0.04
All students	11,044	$10.65	11,663	$9.72	$0.93

*A positive difference indicates that graduates earn more than leavers. A negative difference indicates leavers earn more than graduates.

Median: Half the students earn more than the wage and half less.

Source: SBCTC Data Warehouse: DL-Jobs. Wages reported for all former students with UI covered employment in Washington State at six to nine months after college.

We conclude that it is appropriate to provide incentives for colleges to increase the percentage of programs that offer the typical graduate higher wages. Recent special funding for a laid-off worker program provided dollars for colleges that would start new programs for high-wage, high-demand jobs. Currently, one aspect of the state's performance-funding system rewards efforts to increase the percentage of students in these higher wage job programs. Because students of color are more likely than whites to be in the lower wage job areas, the state board has established a goal to increase the percentage of students of color in higher wage programs.

Potential Areas for New Knowledge. The DLOA allows us to test the *value-add* of college because it is possible to determine the gain in earnings after training compared to before college. One of the first patterns observed in looking at this value-add is that students with low earnings before college tend to enroll in the lower wage occupational programs. These students have higher wages after college than before, but the after-college wages continue to be relatively low compared to other students. Our data show that the typical degree or certificate student in the high-wage programs earned $10 to $11 an hour before college whereas the typical degree or certificate student in the low wage programs earned less than $8 an hour before college. Washington community and technical college staff are just now looking at these findings and asking whether students track themselves into the programs rather than taking advantage of the whole range of program opportunities available to them.

Choices Made as Data Become Information

To create a DLOA that is easy to use to translate data into information, the SBCTC and our partners made many data-related decisions. The key design choices are described here.

Indexing Quarters. Data in the UI wage file are stored by calendar quarter. For example, the UI wage file in all states contains the amount earned at a firm by an individual for an entire quarter. For each individual, the DLOA collapses the earnings from all firms in the same quarter. As described earlier, these combined earnings are indexed related to the student's beginning and ending of college. In this way the DLOA provides a convenient way to report the combined earnings quickly of all graduates for a given period after college, before college, or during college.

A key decision in any follow-up process is selection of the appropriate period after college for gathering outcomes. Our choice is to report posttraining outcomes for the third quarter after training. Our research indicates that most community and technical college graduates are able to move into the kinds of jobs consistent with their level of training by the third quarter. Prior to that time, most former students are employed, but many continue their college job while waiting for results from licensure exams or waiting for an employer to select candidates from the available pool. For June 1998 graduates, for example, the third quarter after training is January to March 1999 or approximately six to nine months after college. Although we also are interested in looking at a full year of earnings after college, the delay in waiting for data for the third through the sixth quarter after college limits our use of such data. Since earnings for students do not show significant value-add in the first and second quarter after college, we do not look at the first-to-fourth-quarter data.

The indexing of quarters is an improvement over the system SBCTC used before DLOA. In the past, to reduce costs we chose to link college records to a single UI quarter. We had selected the January to March period in the year after college. This choice represented the third quarter for June graduates, the largest single group in the exiting class (typically 48 percent of those graduating or leaving college in a given year). For summer graduates, however, the January to March period was a year and a half after college.

Reporting Earnings, Hours, and Hourly Wages. We have elected to describe median earnings, wage, and hour data rather than the mean. Earnings and, to a lesser extent, hours do not follow a normal curve. Most students earn wages below $15 an hour during the third quarter after college. Some, however, earn $30, $40, even $70 an hour when all earnings, including bonus wages, are included. The median value most accurately describes the typical wage rate for a pattern like that shown in Figure 3.2.

Inflation-Adjusted Dollars. We often want to look at earnings over time, so it is important to look at inflation-adjusted data. To meet that need, the DLOA system includes both the actual hourly wage rate and quarterly earnings and inflation-adjusted wages and earnings. We use the implicit price deflator to translate actual dollars into a 1992 value. Researchers then use a table of price factors (contained in the DLOA) to translate the stored 1992 value into current inflation-adjusted value. In this chapter, the data are shown in 1997 dollars, for example.

Pre-Post Analysis. The DLOA allows analysis of earnings after training compared to the pretraining earnings. The pre- and post-training earnings comparisons allow us to look at the value-add of college education. We have agreed to report this comparison for the third quarter before college compared to the third quarter after college, comparing only those with earnings in both the before and after period.

Small Numbers. The DLOA allows the aggregation of results from several years' data or for several related programs. We have found that aggregation is necessary to achieve our goal of providing representative employment and earnings data, that is, data that vary year to year only as a reflection of changes in the extent to which the program meets employer needs. To achieve this end, the data must vary based on what happens to the group, not because of individual student choice. We have found that the behavior of a few individuals influence the data for programs with fewer than 100 students. Unfortunately, most programs are smaller than 100. To compensate for the small numbers, we report data for all similar programs in the state combined, combine several related programs, or combine data from two or more years.

Summary

A decade of use of unemployment insurance data has resulted in new knowledge to inform our policy decisions related to vocational education. This use

**Figure 3.2. Wage Pattern of Graduates and Leavers
(1995–96 Cohort) in 1992 Dollars**

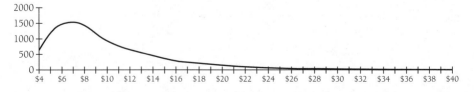

of the administrative employment records goes considerably beyond meeting reporting requirements for program review. We use our conclusions to direct resources to areas that need improvement and to share information on the strengths of the college system.

We have used our new knowledge to support our claim that students who stay long enough to complete their program fare well in the job market. At the same time, the finding that leavers are employed at lower rates and with less increase in hourly earnings compared with graduates has challenged us to reduce the number of students who leave programs long before completing their training.

The most challenging policy issue stemming from the new knowledge relates to the programs that consistently result in low wages (less than $9 an hour for graduates). Since high school graduates without the investment in college can obtain these wages, the question arises as to whether colleges should provide training in these programs. Regardless of the answer to that question, we conclude that it is appropriate to provide incentives for colleges to increase the percentage of programs that offer the typical graduate higher wages. Special funding has been available to start new high-wage, high-demand job programs.

What we have learned about low-wage occupations has helped us direct our policy related to welfare reform. Based on the knowledge that employment rates increase with training, we have selected to focus on training welfare participants with less than a high school education. Adults without high school training typically have low rates of employment, as shown in Figure 3.1. If these adults can be trained for high-demand, albeit low-wage jobs, they will increase their employment level and thus their level of earnings over time. Further, we are coupling this strategy with a focus on further training in middle and higher-wage programs for welfare participants after they gain employment. This strategy to increase earnings over time through part-time enrollment while working was informed by the insights gained from our use of unemployment insurance data.

References

Grubb, W. N. *The Returns to Education and Training in the Sub-Baccalaureate Labor Market: Evidence from the Survey of Income and Program Participation 1984–1990.* Berkeley, Calif.: National Center for Research in Vocational Education, 1995. (MDS–765)

Kane, T., and Rouse, C. E. *Labor Market Returns to Two- and Four-Year Colleges: Is a Credit a Credit and Do Degrees Matter?* Cambridge, Mass.: National Bureau of Economic Research, Inc., 1993. (Working Paper no. 4268)

Mortenson, T. G. "Employment and Unemployment Rates by Educational Attainment 1970–1996." *Postsecondary Education Opportunity,* 1997, 62, 1–14.

Seppanen, L. J. "Linkages to the World of Employment." In P. Ewell (ed.), *Student Tracking: New Techniques, New Demands.* New Directions for Institutional Research, no 87. San Francisco: Jossey-Bass, 1995.

State Board for Community and Technical Colleges (SBCTC). *Workforce Employment and Training Act: Second Year Accountability Report for Training Programs,* HB 1988. Olympia: Washington State Board for Community and Technical Colleges SBCTC, 1995. (ED 392 473)

Stevens, D. W., and Shi, J. *New Perspectives on Documenting Employment and Earnings Outcomes in Vocational Education.* Berkeley, Calif.: National Center for Research in Vocational Education, 1996. (ED 399 398)

Washington State Workforce Training and Education Coordinating Board (WTECB). *Workforce Training Results: An Evaluation of Washington State's Workforce Training System,* Second Edition. Olympia: Washington State Workforce Training and Education Coordinating Board, 1997.

Westat, Inc. "Net Impact Evaluation of Retraining Under ESHB 1988." Paper prepared for the Washington Workforce Training and Education Coordinating Board, Olympia, Wash., 1997.

LORETTA SEPPANEN is the senior research manager at the Washington State Board for Community and Technical Colleges, Olympia, Washington.

This chapter discusses the collaboration among the California Community Colleges Chancellor's Office, the California Employment Development Department, and community college practitioners to develop an administrative data-matching system to meet accountability mandates. The chapter delineates the many benefits of collaboration when matching student records with records from other administrative databases and examines how completeness of external databases can affect outcomes.

Collaborative Administrative Record Matching in California

W. Charles Wiseley

California community colleges (CCC), like college systems in every state, have accountability legislation to which they must respond. Prior to the 1990s, most of the accountability reporting requirements were met by the individual colleges in the CCC system. Colleges either sent reports directly to the coordinating agency requiring the report or to the CCC chancellor's office for packaging into a single statewide report. Both the state and the chancellor's office recognized the need for a systematic way of meeting the increasingly burdensome reporting requirements. The chancellor's office and the CCC began implementing a data system in 1989 to consolidate efforts to respond to legislative accountability mandates on the 107 colleges in the system. Under the new data system, colleges submit detailed course enrollment and student demographic data to the chancellor's office. These data are then aggregated to meet the state and federal reporting requirements.

Accountability legislation typically has many aspects of accountability that may include measures of inputs, processes, outputs, and outcomes. Most of the data available for accountability from the new chancellor's office data system address the input, processes, and output measures in legislative reporting requirements of access, successful course completion, retention, degrees conferred, and so forth.

Both state and federal bodies, however, have mandated accountability systems that include outcome measures. Two pieces of federal legislation, in particular, the Carl D. Perkins Vocational and Applied Technology Education Act (1990) and the Student Right to Know Act (1996), have mandated outcome measures that require data not typically available from a college where a student attended. Because the new chancellor's office data system did include student Social Security numbers (SSNs), however, tracking students in administrative databases outside community colleges where SSN were used as a unique identifier was possible. Linking the chancellor's office database with external administrative databases has provided useful information for specific outcomes contained in each separate external matching source. Each external database, however, usually addresses only one possible outcome. Multiple external sources are required to provide as complete a picture of student flow as possible. Gaps in outcome data for specific groups may produce extremely negative consequences for those groups.

This chapter discusses the collaboration required among state agencies, higher education segments, and college practitioners to meet the Carl D. Perkins Act mandates for accountability. Moreover, it delineates the many benefits of collaboration when matching student records with records from other administrative databases and examines how completeness of external databases can affect outcomes. Past and present collaborative efforts have provided and continue to provide California community colleges with information for accountability purposes and, more important, information useful for instructional improvement and enhancement of student services.

Collaborative Requirements in the Carl D. Perkins Act

The federal Carl D. Perkins Act passed in 1990 not only had specific requirements for an accountability system but included requirements for a collaborative process. Those requirements specified that a committee of practitioners (COP) would be formed to develop outcome measures and performance standards to inform vocational education practitioners about their programs. In California, where both the K–12 and community college systems offer vocational education, the COP membership included California Department of Education (CDE) representatives, K–12 district staff and teachers, and California community college staff and practitioners. The COP had a wide range of interests represented and soon developed into two groups that could focus on the measurement systems available to the two different entities of adult vocational education under CDE and community college vocational education. The community college members included the chancellor's office dean of vocational education, a vocational education specialist from the chancellor's office, and eighteen college vocational deans and faculty members. After developing numerous measures, the California community college section of the COP determined that it would begin with the three measures for which data were available or could be developed in the near future: achievement, retention, and placement.

Data for the achievement and retention measures were available directly from the California Community Colleges Chancellor's Office Management Information System (COMIS) database, which had its first phase fully implemented by the fall of 1991. Although the COMIS database contains a wide variety of information, such as student demographics, enrollments, grades, student services received, staff and faculty demographics, assignments, salaries, and facilities, the COMIS did not contain any information on student placement after college or any data that would allow follow up via traditional survey methodologies, such as student mailing address and complete name.

Traditional follow-up surveys were being conducted at the individual colleges but few standards were in place for either the data collected on those surveys or the methodologies used to collect the data. California community colleges had been doing some student flow tracking by matching student records with the student record data in the other higher education segments in the region (that is, University of California, California State University, Association of Independent Colleges and Universities, and the University of Nevada). Those data matches were occurring sporadically in California through efforts of researchers at the colleges, the information systems staff at the chancellor's office, and through California's Intersegmental Coordinating Counsel (ICC) data needs task force.

Using education databases to track student flow through and within higher education segments does not inform us about or tell us where the majority of community college students go when they leave the college—into the workforce. A consistent, objective, and low-cost method to follow up that majority of students who did not immediately continue in public higher education in California was needed.

Matching Administrative Student Records with the UI Database

A few states were leading the way toward doing student follow-up in a not so traditional way. Matching student leaver records with administrative databases collected for other purposes such as unemployment insurance (UI) and military and federal payrolls was increasingly providing very high match or return rates for follow-up studies for community colleges in Florida (Pfeiffer, 1990), Texas (Froeschle, 1991), Washington (Seppanen, 1993), and other states.

California Community Colleges Chancellor's Office commissioned a feasibility study in 1991 to determine whether matching student leaver records with the California UI administrative database would provide the same useful low-cost follow-up information experienced in the other states matching with UI systems. The Employment Development Department (EDD), who maintains California's UI database, was contacted by the chancellor's office, and contracts were developed with Dr. Jack Friedlander at Santa Barbara City College to conduct the study and with EDD to do the UI base-wage file matching with community college student records.

Early matches used cohorts of students who had either left the college system or completed degree or certificate programs prior to 1993. The match of COMIS student records to employment records in the UI base-wage file was accomplished electronically and involved the following general procedures:

CCC creates a file of student SSNs from the COMIS where the student either received a degree or certificate (completers) or did not return to any community college in the CCC for one year (leavers) following a cohort year.

CCC submits a file of completer and leaver SSNs to EDD for matching with the UI wage records.

EDD appends quarterly wage record data for the prior year to the SSNs submitted for matching.

Student records with wage data appended are returned to the chancellor's office.

To acquire longitudinal data, each completer/leaver cohort is resubmitted to EDD for matching until a four-year span of wages is accumulated at the chancellor's office.

The California Collaborative Working Group

As the feasibility study progressed and began to show promise, an advisory committee, the Vocational Education Technical Advisory Research and Accountability Committee (RAC), was developed to determine the best methodology for assessing the benefit of community college attendance given the constraints of the available data. The RAC needed to assess how the deficiencies of both the UI database and the COMIS would affect the outcomes being measured when the project was expanded to include more colleges. The RAC, to meet this charge, needed to include members beyond chancellor's office and EDD staff, and brought in college faculty, administrators, and researchers in the development of the reports to address the COP's placement measure. This was the beginning of the expansion of the collaboration beyond the chancellor's office and EDD.

Understanding and documenting details such as where the UI data would not provide employment information (for example, self-employed, military, federal employment) and where the COMIS could not provide accurate information (for example, formal program participation, complete enrollment history) required a broad range of participants in the collaboration process. Although the estimates of those employed but not represented in the UI wage records was only 3 percent nationally (Friedlander, 1996; Stevens, Richmond, Haenn, and Michie, 1992), concerns were raised that questioned the composition of the California labor force as well as the impact on specific college program outcomes for those groups not represented. During the course of the feasibility study and following implementations, the collaboration among EDD, the chancellor's office, and the college practitioners grew ever more important in understanding the data shortcomings as the reports became more refined and results began to be made available for public scrutiny. Without the concerted efforts of the participants, the development of methodologies to provide meaningful data and useful reports would have taken many more months, possibly even years, longer to accomplish. Six years into the study, the collaborative process continues to inform the committees and helps us refine the reports to develop new understandings of subpopulations, such as traditional degree-seeking students, students returning for skill upgrading or license maintenance, or economically disadvantaged students, in the follow-up reports.

The UI database contained employment records for 80 percent of the student completers and leavers during their last year in college from the two colleges in the feasibility study (Friedlander, 1993). When considering the needs for follow-up in the Carl D. Perkins Act that the feasibility study was testing, however, a number of deficiencies in California's UI base-wage file system were illuminated as well as some deficiencies in the COMIS.

The Working Group's Challenge

To follow up students who left the community colleges and provide useful information to faculty, administrators, and policy makers, some very basic information needed to be defined by the RAC. In concept, the simple question to answer was, Is there an economic benefit for attendance at a California community college?, or more specifically, Is there an economic benefit for attendance in a *vocational program* at a California community college? Two basic pieces of information were required to operationalize this measure indicating possible benefit for community college attendance: (1) the vocational program the student was in college attending, and (2) the impact on earnings that program may have had. The operationalization of these concepts was seen to be problematic, given the available data, for the reasons indicated below.

First, unlike senior universities in California and like community college systems in many other states, no formal acceptance for entry into a program of study is required for most programs offered at California community colleges. Entrance into any California community college is open to anyone who can benefit, whether the student is a high school graduate or not (some health care profession programs such as nursing do require formal acceptance). Moreover, no date of acceptance into the college is collected in the COMIS; therefore, data to determine program entry date could not be determined until a sufficient number of years were available in the COMIS.

Program of study could easily be identified for those students receiving certificates or degrees, since the program is identified as the program in which an award is conferred, which is reported in the COMIS as well as the type of award (for example, AA, AS, two-year certificate). The value of community colleges, however, with missions that address life-long learning, skill upgrading, license maintenance, and so forth, would be understated by tracking only completers. Efforts were started to identify programs using student course-taking behavior that would allow leavers not earning or receiving degrees or certificates to be included in the study. With the additional leaver information, programs could better use the reports to evaluate their impact on different populations of students. Identifying a concentration of enrollments in a program area of sufficient quantity to justify evaluating the program based on those enrollments was identified as a pseudo-indicator of program. For the feasibility study, leavers, completers who left the institution for at least one year, and those completing but not leaving were followed.

Next, impact on wages using after-college earnings require a baseline for comparison. Without before-college earnings, since no beginning college date for establishing a before-college period was available, last-year-in-college earnings and first-year-out-of-college earnings were determined to be useful comparative baselines for third-year-out-of-college earnings, depending on the population to be examined.

Unlike Florida, Texas, Washington, and other states, California does not collect any data from employers other than gross quarterly earnings that could be used to calculate hourly wage such as hours worked per week, weeks worked in the quarter, or even data to determine full-time/part-time status. No job title or occupational classification indicators or even county of employment were available in the California UI data.

Working closely with EDD staff, chancellor's office staff began to investigate the possibility of expanding the amount of data collected from employers in an employer survey pilot project. From that pilot, CCC found that a majority of employers would not provide that additional data. Those findings were similar to the findings of a study funded by the California Occupational Information Coordinating Committee (COICC) in the late 1980s to examine the possibility of expanding the amount of data collected from employers in the quarterly reports to EDD to include some of those data types. Employers were overwhelmingly opposed to any expansion of the data required on the quarterly statements to EDD or in a supplemental survey. Specifically, smaller businesses saw it as an additional burden that could not be justified. In the pro-business, less-government political atmosphere of California in the 1980s and 1990s, that burden was seen as sufficient cause to abandon any efforts to expand the data collection for the UI system.

Without some indicator of time worked for the earnings reported, no comparable figure such as hourly wage or even classification of full-time/part-time status was available. Comparing gross wages for any amount of work such as part-time or partial quarter seemed invalid, and alternative methods of estimating annual earnings were considered and tested. Decisions were made to use the median of gross wages for those working in all four quarters as well as a proxy measure for full-time employment. The proxy measure for full-time employment was chosen to allow a more reliable figure for comparing earnings from year to year when looking at earning gains. The standard labor market figure for average manufacturing wage in 1991 was used to approximate full-time employment. The figure $12,875, half the average manufacturing wage (about $5.50/hour), was considered full-time/full-year employment for the study.

As the feasibility study came to a close and sufficient information was available to support a belief that the project was not only feasible but cost-effective and would produce information currently available in no other forum, the decision to continue the project was made. The RAC, chaired by Jack Friedlander, first had to address the following basic questions in order to expand the study systemwide: How do we identify the vocational program that will be evaluated based on student leaver employment and earnings? What earnings should be used as the baseline for comparison until we can identify program entry date? Can we identify program entry date without new data collection? When is a student considered a leaver?

The committee worked diligently, pouring over the methodology and conclusions of the feasibility study, and provided invaluable advice for the implementation of the next step—the pilot.

The next study commissioned by the chancellor's office was a pilot conducted by Jack Friedlander in 1993 with eighteen colleges. The linking of the COMIS and UI databases returned the same high match rate and provided a wealth of information to the practitioners at the colleges (Friedlander, 1996).

The Challenge of Implementation Systemwide

The advisory committee, working with the information from the pilot study, began discussions to refine the reports for implementation systemwide. Categories of students, such as *vocational student, skill upgrade student,* and *enrollment concentration,* and program assignment methodologies were redefined at the RAC's direction. Additional links were made to the California State University (CSU) system to reclassify those students as continuing their education at CSU and to remove them from the earnings calculations.

Systemwide implementation began in 1996 with the publication of the 1990–1991 leaver cohort draft reports, which included 100 colleges submitting SSNs as unique identifiers to the COMIS. Six months later, in early 1997, after review and further refinement, the first annual report following the 1991–1992 leaver cohort was published.

As of January 1998, California Community Colleges has matched six leaver cohorts with the California EDD's UI base-wage file and the first three cohorts, 1990–1991, 1991–1992, and 1992–1993, with the CSU system. The system set up to provide reports from the matches had to meet federal Privacy Act restrictions and is much more complex than the data matching itself. Even though California Community Colleges contracted with EDD to do the matching as research on our behalf, all of the Family Education Rights and Privacy Act (FERPA) caveats and restrictions had to be observed. Contracting with EDD facilitated the cooperation and support of the staff at EDD to help us understand and meet the constraints put on EDD to meet federal Privacy Act and California Unemployment Insurance Code (sections 1094 and 1095) requirements.

Median annual earnings while in college, one year after college, and three years after college, as well as median earnings gain for those years, were now available on reports with certain privacy-based restrictions and caveats. The reports were designed to inform faculty of the levels of employment their former students were entering into and any increases in earnings for those students over a four-year span. It has become very clear in the past few years that this information can be invaluable for instructional improvement at the local level and is the most effective use of the data available through the UI base-wage file matches. The objective employment information regarding entry level wages of students and the earning gains over the following years provide insights to faculty about program acceptance in the workplace that are available from no other venue.

Only through collaborative efforts with faculty and faculty's interaction with the employers in the local economies, however, can we understand the complexities of the data coming out of the base-wage file research as we develop standardized reports. For example, movement of major segments of job categories into temporary or independent contractor status will have great impact on certain programs in different economic areas when UI wage data are used to determine employment outcomes. Faculty need to be aware of those conditions to prepare their students for the workplace, and report readers need to be apprised of the labor market conditions for those programs to properly interpret the outcomes in the reports. For this reason, collaborative systems to facilitate communication among employers, faculty, report developers, and the policy makers who read those reports need to be institutionalized.

The Collaborative Process Helps Highlight Problems

Through the efforts of the vocational deans, staff, and faculty participating in the RAC we began to understand that aggregating outcomes derived from the UI base-wage files for programs at a college level may be problematic. Although the aggregation may provide sufficient numbers for valid analysis and inference, the aggregation of unlike programs removed some reliability. For example, nursing programs may include both LVN and RN programs, which have very different outcome expectations (that is, annual income). Aggregating outcomes to a general nursing category therefore would mask those programs, and any comparison between colleges would be directly influenced by the proportion of RN students in the nursing program. Aggregating to higher levels such as nursing statewide would have the same RN ratio influence. Therefore, using aggregations above the college level where local practitioners understand program content can only make sense where programs across institutions have similar core curriculum and outcome goals and objectives for their students.

In California, with few exceptions, the curriculum is not standardized among colleges or universities in the same system or even colleges in the same district. Through cooperative efforts between college practitioners, chancellor's office staff, and EDD staff, measures were constructed that allowed a more valid consolidation of program outcomes across colleges by examining student workload completed and awards conferred. Additional work is being done to differentiate between certificate programs requiring less than two years (less than sixty units) and those lasting two or more years (sixty or more semester units).

Benefits of Including EDD staff on the RAC

The efforts of the EDD staff were invaluable in working with the EDD information security office to develop a trusting relationship. Report development proceeded smoothly with little actual monitoring of the project other than review at the RAC meetings. EDD staff participated in the project's advisory committee to advise CCC research staff of many of the deficiencies of the UI base-wage file, the UI data collection and storage mechanisms, and changes in those systems. Committee participation facilitated EDD's availability for quick additional research to provide information such as employers' reticence to report any additional information. EDD also provided links to other research entities using the UI base-wage files for research, thus helping community colleges develop a deeper understanding of the composition, participant attrition, and other complexities of the UI base-wage file and its contents. EDD staff continue to work on expanding the linkages to other administrative databases, such as the military and federal payroll systems, to increase our knowledge of the 20 percent we don't find in the UI base-wage and CSU enrollment files.

California Community Colleges continues to collaborate with EDD in initiating new studies to complement the UI follow-up reports with relatedness to training measures, and in developing lists of occupations of program leavers and local employers of program leavers. Having EDD staff intimately involved with these projects also meets EDD's need to monitor the project to see that our reporting and handling of the data meet their privacy and UI code requirements.

Policy, Privacy, and Resources

Requirements for unitary data matching have policy, privacy, and resource considerations. The general counsels from all of the data matching sources were involved to assure compliance with FERPA and other privacy legislation and regulations. The basic barriers that the educational institutions face when matching student educational records with records from other data sources are those that protect the privacy of every person in the United States. Additionally, however, educational institutions must meet the requirements of FERPA when disclosing student records to any individual or entity. FERPA does, however, allow disclosure of student records for research under the exception of instructional improvement.

The task of responding to accountability requirements and meeting the requirements of FERPA can only be accomplished with cooperative efforts between institutions that minimize disclosure of student records and maximize the ability to relate the outcomes to instruction. Any cooperative effort between educational institutions and entities outside education must keep the management of privacy breach risks as the highest priority. By developing the appropriate cohorts and reporting levels that meet instructional improvement requirements, executing detailed contracts, and building relationships between institutional liaisons for research, report approval, and monitoring, Privacy Act considerations can be met while constructing accountability systems.

Adhering to the constraints of privacy legislation does not address policy implications of information provided by the UI base-wage file research. Full cooperation of faculty administering programs at the college level is required to understand student flow into the workplace. Policy makers must be made aware of how the outcomes may be affected by the deficiencies in the UI base-wage file. Local-level participation is necessary in the development of reports and in the reporting of findings for this awareness to be realized. Coordination and cooperation must be ongoing and provide for communication pathways among faculty, researchers, and policy makers.

Once college staff began using the reports to understand the outcomes of students in their programs, researchers began requesting access to the unitary earnings data. College-level research that tests whether specific intervention strategies had an impact on student earnings or placement might more directly inform college staff. Privacy restrictions of FERPA and California UI code restrictions, however, under current uses of available technology, set constraints on local college access to unitary UI wage data.

Without being able to provide college access to unitary outcomes data, human resources at the chancellor's office for implementing and monitoring projects have been strained. New avenues for communication such as e-mail, video conferencing, e-mail discussion lists, teleconferences, video phones, and other electronic media as well as the high-power, low-cost computing resources becoming available will help the chancellor's office meet the expanding information needs of college staff and policy makers with increased timeliness.

We Are Still Learning

The California Community Colleges Chancellor's Office continues to pursue avenues that will focus resources on collecting, analyzing, and disseminating new information to college researchers and faculty as we learn new lessons through the collaborative process. As California government moves closer to performance-based funding for community colleges and noneducation workforce development boards develop outcome measures on which to base that funding, the collaboration and the lessons we have learned through it in the past few years become invaluable. The lessons continue as the chancellor's office and other collaborative working groups sift through comments from over eighty college staff and faculty researching how to better identify which program to assign students who complete varying degrees of course work but do not complete degree or certificate requirements so that instruction can be more directly related to the outcomes. Those collaborative efforts among college faculty, researchers, the CCC chancellor's office, and EDD are helping to develop a new understanding of outcomes by using the UI base-wage and other data and determining their relationship to instruction and educational services provided at the colleges.

References

Friedlander, J. *Using Wage Record Data to Track the Post-College Employment and Earnings of Community College Students.* Santa Barbara, Calif.: Santa Barbara City College, 1993. (ED 360 007)

Friedlander, J. *Using Wage Record Data to Track the Post-College Employment Rates and Wages of California Community College Students.* Santa Barbara, Calif.: Santa Barbara City College, 1996. (ED 390 507)

Froeschle, R. *Pilot Study Findings of the Use of the Texas Employment Commission Unemployment Insurance Wage Records to Document Outcomes of Technical-Vocational Education and Training.* Austin: Texas Higher Education Coordinating Board, 1991.

Pfeiffer, J. J. *Florida Education and Training Placement Program.* Annual Report. Tallahassee: Florida Department of Education, 1990.

Seppanen, L. J. *Using Administrative Data Matches for Follow-Up.* Technical Report No. 93-5. Olympia: Washington State Board for Community and Technical Colleges, 1993. (ED 382 250)

Stevens, D. W., Richmond, P. A., Haenn, J. F., and Michie, J. S. *Measuring Outcomes Using Unemployment Insurance Wage Records.* Washington, D.C.: Research and Evaluation Associates, 1992.

W. CHARLES WISELEY is information systems specialist, California Community Colleges Chancellor's Office, Sacramento, California.

In the early 1990s, attention focused on the role of the North Carolina community college system in workforce development. Efforts were put forth to establish and develop measurable outcomes of successful workforce training, particularly employment rates, median salary of program completers, and completers' satisfaction with programs and colleges. This chapter presents the latest findings regarding state efforts in economic development and the contributions of community colleges.

Measurable Outcomes of Workforce Development and the Economic Impact of Attending a North Carolina Community College

Larry W. Gracie

State-based performance indicators for higher education are rapidly becoming the hallmark of the 1990s. By 1994 over one-third of the states had some form of performance indicator legislation enacted (Bogue, Creech, and Folger, 1993). With each legislative session since, the number has increased. In North Carolina, discussions at the state level are beginning to shift toward funding the educational enterprise based on outcomes, effectiveness, and efficiency (Gaither, Nedwek, and Neal, 1994). Recently, the Southern Regional Education Board data exchange papers illustrated that North Carolina collects a greater number of *accountability or performance measures* than the other twelve reporting Southern states (Marks, 1997). North Carolina produces forty reports concerning these measures whereas the average for the thirteen reporting states is slightly greater than eighteen reports.

This chapter discusses North Carolina's measurable outcomes of workforce development and the economic impact of attending a community college in the state. More specifically, it presents the comprehensive reporting system along with a discussion about using the data inform policy.

North Carolina Higher Education System

North Carolina's public higher education system comprises fifty-eight community colleges and sixteen state universities. The community college system and the university system are governed by separate boards. The State Board of Community Colleges, the Board of Governors of the University of North Carolina system, and the State Board of Education's joint participation form the State Education Commission. The governor convenes this joint commission to review common educational agenda items.

Under the management and leadership of the State Board of Community Colleges, the board adopts and implements statewide policy on the establishment, administration, and operation of institutions; the allocation and expenditure of state and federal funds; the acquisition and disposal of property; the admission of students; the establishment of tuition and fees; the awarding of degrees, diplomas, and certificates; and the requirements for college transfer programs and other curricular and course offerings. At the local level, community colleges are governed by a board of trustees that is statutorily designated as the local administrative board of the college.

Educational and Economic Development Policies

During the late 1980s and early 1990s, North Carolina's higher education system moved from simply reporting quantitative measures to a period of accountability, qualitative reviews of programs and services with outcome measures, and, finally, performance budgeting. A comprehensive review of all North Carolina state governmental agencies was conducted under the precept of Government Performance Audit Committee. During this period, a number of task forces were established and legislative policies were developed. The Accountability Task Force's charge was to develop institutional performance standards on critical success factors and to develop a model for colleges to use for measuring institutional effectiveness. In 1989, the General Assembly mandated that "the State Board of Community Colleges shall develop a *Critical Success Factors* list to define statewide measures of accountability for all community colleges" (SL 1989; C. 752; S. 80).

In 1993, state legislation mandated that the State Board of Community Colleges develop performance standards for appropriate critical success factors and develop a model for colleges to use in determining institutional effectiveness (Senate Bill 27, Section 109). At that time, the State Board of Community Colleges adopted a new set of system goals that included a goal on "Accountability and Standards" (State Board Retreat, September 9, 1993). In the 1995 state appropriations bill, the legislature directed the Office of State Budget and Management to employ the Common Follow-up Management Information System to evaluate the effectiveness of the state's job training, education, and placement programs. These actions to establish standards within critical measures of higher education and the current reporting system are under ongoing legislative review. During the summer of 1998, Senate Bill 1366 was introduced as a special provision to ensure a higher degree of program accountability and establish appropriate levels of performance for each measure based on sound methodological practices (Section 10.5). The provision states that "the State Board shall develop an action plan to improve the timeliness and accuracy of the data that are required to be reported by each institution. This plan may include withholding state funds from the institution if an institution is not in compliance" (Section 10.8). This proposal represents a new, expanding governing role for the North Carolina community college system. If not adopted at this time, the proposal is likely to be included in future legislation.

North Carolina's Current Reporting System

Each accountability and performance report must be examined as a part of the comprehensive outcome measures system. One strength of the North Carolina reporting system is its use of multivariable collection systems. Conversely, one weakness is the mutable variables collected. The initial result of the reporting system illustrates the importance of how these data are collected, which is influenced by the *perceived intended* level of use and purpose. As campus staff observe the use of these data in program evaluation or funding, their attention to these policies increases significantly. A review (beyond the recent legislative initiative noted earlier) within the North Carolina community college system is now being conducted to investigate which reports can be collapsed into a future reporting platform.

Critical Success Factors. Current Critical Success Factors consist of seven critical factors and thirty-three measures of program success. This report is prepared annually and submitted to the State Board of Community Colleges and the General Assembly as a testimony to the health and performance of the system. A recent presentation to the Joint Education Appropriations Subcommittee proposed dividing the Critical Success Factors report into two parts: a common core of indicators of success, and measures of progress toward objectives. The minutes of the current Community College System Planning Council reflect that the state's Critical Success Factors merger with the American Association of Community Colleges (AACC) core indicators are being investigated. Developing benchmarks beyond the North Carolina community college system for further analysis is deemed desirable.

Annual Programs Review. The current Annual Programs Review's precursor was first referenced as *desktop audit* or *annual program audit,* and the system office initiated procedures to automate program review reporting in 1996. The Community College System's Annual Programs Review is divided between outcome measures from the vocational-technical, college transfer, and continuing education sectors. These data are collected for college completers and noncompleters on program and college satisfaction, goal attainment and employment rates, and from employers on their satisfaction with community college graduates. Each campus is encouraged to use the Annual Programs Review to collect additional information on institutional effectiveness.

Each program is evaluated on its success at meeting at least five of these eight criteria. Currently, successful performance standards are set 15 percent below the system respondents. Table 5.1 illustrates the 1998 outcomes based on our 1997 survey responses.

In addition, each training program that has a *licensure rate* is measured against the standard for that profession. If the licensure rate on four out of eight standards listed in Table 5.1 is below the established standard, the program is

Table 5.1. Annual Programs Review Scorecard and Standards for 1998

	Population	Measure	Respondents	Standard
1.	Completers and Non-completers	Three-year head count Enrollment average		10/year
2.	Completers	Goal attainment	98.6%	83.8%
3.	Non-completers	Goal attainment	72.5%	61.6%
4.	Completers	Program satisfaction	89.2%	75.8%
5.	Non-completers	Program satisfaction	83.3%	70.8%
6.	Completers	Employment rate	87.7%	72.7%
7.	Non-completers	Employment rate	74.5%	63.3%
8.	Employers	Satisfaction	91.3%	77.6%

subject to an additional review. Additional reviews may terminate a program that does not develop a plan to bring the program within these performance measures.

Common Follow-up System. The first sets of meaningful data are being produced at this time. The Common Follow-up System has grown to become a complete collection of records of individual enrollments in education, training, and placement programs plus demographics and unemployment insurance (UI) wages for individuals before, during, and after training. The Common Follow-up System data are provided to participating agencies with information on the wages and other agency involvement of their students/customers/program participants over a five-year period. In addition to the Community College System (CCS), eight governmental agencies are participating in this process: the Department of Public Instruction (DPI), the university system (UNC), the Department of Labor (DOL), Vocational Rehabilitation (VOC RE), Division of Employment and Training (EM/TRA), Social Services (SS), and Employment Security Commission (ESC). Table 5.2 illustrates this year's relationship of agencies' participation in mutable programs.

The quality of these data are increasing with every collection attempt. At this point, approximately 84 percent of the community college participants were found to be in the unemployment insurance (UI) database. These UI data are available for a five-year period, which allows for review of earnings before, during, and after program participation.

Community college students also participate in other programs designed to assist in state workforce development. The complementary nature of these programs, illustrated in Table 5.2, has encouraged the consideration of *Return on Investment* (ROI) models (Brayson, 1996). Though a ROI model has not been agreed upon, it can be seen that the North Carolina community college system has collaborated with many in the workforce development effort. In many ways, community college participation has been a major component of other workforce development agencies' assistance or training plans to prepare citizens for the workforce.

Table 5.2. State Agencies Workforce Development Program Relationships, 1998

	DPI	CCS	UNC	DOL	VOC RE	EM/TRA	SS	ESC
DPI		1.54%	0.20%	11.32%	6.35%	19.80%	1.95%	1.49%
CCS	5.12%		8.95%	35.53%	27.38%	44.95%	28.48%	16.05%
UNC	0.18%	2.53%		0.84%	4.47%	2.17%	1.73%	2.40%
DOL	0.17%	0.16%	0.01%		0.13%	0.10%	0.05%	0.07%
VOC RE								
EM/TRA	2.85%	1.95%	0.33%	0.98%	3.84%		4.63%	1.59%
SS	0.65%	2.85%	0.61%	1.08%	3.67%	10.67%		3.14%
ESC	7.48%	24.22%	12.81%	23.30%	35.30%	55.07%	47.34%	
N	189,258	627,658	177,472	2,871	37,832	27,275	62,894	947,113

Common Follow-up Data Analysis

The community college system expanded the concept of *completers* and *non-completers* to better illustrate student status and enrollment patterns (Yang and Brown, 1998). For this reporting, classifications for exit completers, exit noncompleters, comeback completers, and comeback noncompleters were established.

Exit noncompleters had the highest earnings after leaving college. However, the mean quarterly earnings of exit completers increased at a faster rate from quarter one to quarter four than the other student status groups (Figure 5.1). The years 1993–1994 and 1994–1995 followed the same pattern as the 1995–1996 data and therefore only the most recent data are reported in Figure 5.1.

Older students had higher annual earnings than younger age groups in each student status group (Figure 5.2). The exit noncompleter had the greatest difference or range of the initial quarter earnings among the selected four age groups. However, exit completers had the highest earnings among all students under age twenty-five (Figure 5.3). The earnings reported by the older age groups (thirty-five to forty-four and over forty-four) illustrate little difference within the comeback completer student status.

An exit completer who earns an AAS degree, diploma, or certificate reports higher quarterly earning than one who earned an associate degree (Figure 5.4). It can be noted that many of the associate degree recipients report that their educational goal includes attending a four-year institution and they may subsequently enroll following their attendance at a community college. The mean quarterly earnings of an AAS degree holder also increase at a faster rate than the other degree holder groups.

In followups on exit completers, the number of hours completed seem to affect both the youngest and oldest of the two age groups established for this study (Figure 5.5).

Figure 5.1. 1995–1996 Mean Quarterly Earnings by Student Status

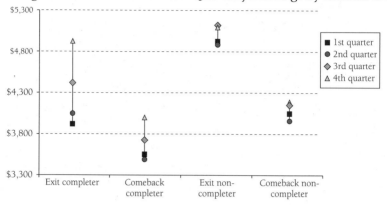

Figure 5.2. 1995–1996 Mean Initial (First) Quarter Earnings by Student Status and Age Group

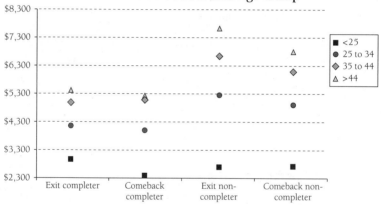

Figure 5.3. 1995–1996 Mean Quarterly Earnings by Student Status for Under Twenty-Five Age Group

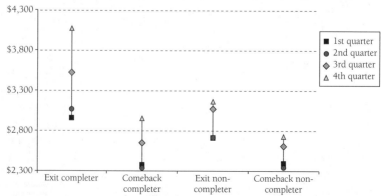

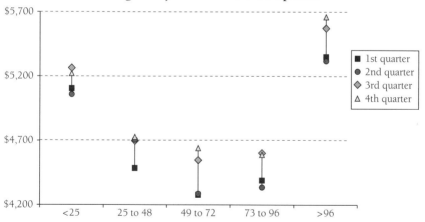

Figure 5.4. 1995–1996 Mean Quarterly Earnings for Student Status "Exit Completer" by Student Outcome

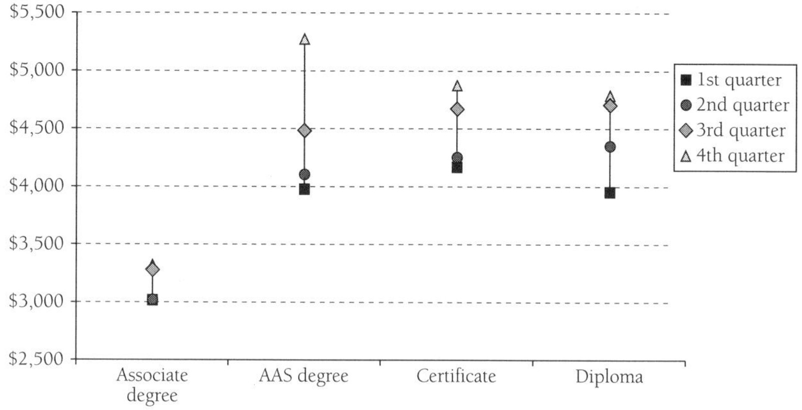

Figure 5.5. 1995–1996 Mean Quarterly Earnings for Student Status "Exit Noncompleter" Enrolled in Two-Year Community College Program by Credit Hours Completed

Conclusion

As with all the measures illustrated here, the true value of the Common Follow-up System lies in potential future studies. As part of these projects, a longitudinal database is being established. This database will allow researchers to track individuals from high school, through higher education, training, and workforce participation. With this information, decision makers will better understand the individual educational and training needs. The cost to the participating governmental agencies and to North Carolina has not been determined to date and is needed to ascertain the value in the future collection of these data items. It is suggested that these accountability and performance measures be reviewed beforehand to help determine whether the resulting data are valuable enough to warrant collection.

These mutable data analysis processes and program outcome measures have already enabled North Carolina to respond quickly to new economic initiatives such as School-to-Work, Tech-Prep, Work-First, Job Ready, and One Stop Centers. The state has also been able to examine participants' costs by program, return on investments, and welfare avoidance in addition to measuring reduction in duplication of effort among the workforce development initiatives. Certainly these capabilities illustrate the value of the North Carolina community college system to the state's economic development efforts. If *adequacy* legal cases move into the community college sector (or any of the governmental sectors participating in these data exchanges), these outcome measures will support the value added to participants of each program.

Future use of these data will fulfill the early goal within accountability legislation of setting clear objectives and strategic plans that require continuous improvement and the study of best practices to meet the need of each client. Ongoing peer review of these data is encouraged. The development of meaningful benchmarks will focus on areas for future improvements. The effectiveness of public sector funds must be examined, and unused or obsolete data elements and reports eliminated. Paramount in any strategic planning process is a *conceptual framework* from which to assess accountability and the need for the public sector agencies to strive for continuous improvement with the use of all funds. The public interest in human capital is enhanced with new efficiency, effectiveness, and performance measures. A test of the value of performance measures and standards will be whether they enhance the quality of the delivery systems or lead to more effective strategic investments in higher education and economic development.

References

Bogue, G., Creech, J., and Folger, J. *Assessing Quality in Higher Education: Policy Actions in SREB States.* Atlanta, Ga.: Southern Regional Education Board, 1993.

Brayson, D. D. *Return on Investment: Guidelines to Determine Workforce Development Impact.* Columbus, Ohio: Minuteman Press, 1996.

Gaither, G., Nedwek, B. P., and Neal, J. E. "Measuring Up: The Promises and Pitfalls of Performance Indicators in Higher Education." *ASHE-ERIC Higher Education Report, 23* (5) 1994.

Marks, J. L. *Proposed Future Data Exchange Indicators.* Atlanta, Ga.: Southern Regional Education Board, 1997.

Yang, X., and Brown, K. "Using Unemployment Insurance Data and Job-Related Data to Track the Employment and Earnings of Community College Students." Paper presented at the annual forum of the Association for Institutional Research, Minneapolis, Minn., May 1998.

LARRY W. GRACIE is associate director for institutional effectiveness planning and research at the North Carolina Community College System, Raleigh, North Carolina.

A college describes its use of earnings data and partnerships to develop new high-wage programs, and identifies issues that emerged in response to a state performance-funding measure tied to professional/technical graduates' earnings.

Partnering to Identify and Support High-Wage Programs

Kae R. Hutchison, Sharon Story Kline, Carol Mandt, Suzanne L. Marks

Of the many challenges facing higher education today, one of the most demanding is how to be responsive to businesses' need for a skilled workforce. Legislatures are spurring colleges to develop responsiveness through emphasis on accountability indicators that require success in job placement or engagement of a greater percentage of students in higher-wage occupations. In the following case study, Bellevue Community College describes three separate but related activities in which wage and job specific accountability indicators play a key role: (1) utilizing partnerships to respond to regional need, (2) identifying and developing high-wage programs, and (3) responding to state accountability measures.

Using Partnerships to Respond to Regional Need

Bellevue Community College (BCC) is a comprehensive, public two-year college serving a group of urban/suburban communities located in the eastern part of the greater Seattle metropolis, an area locally referred to as "the East-side." With a population exceeding 373,000, the Eastside is a major employment center. Home to Microsoft and a burgeoning number of other software companies, along with medical, biotech, telecommunication, and aircraft electronics companies, the Eastside is experiencing increasing demands for a technologically proficient workforce with solid foundation skills (for example, writing, oral communication, critical and mathematical thinking, teamwork).

In 1993, BCC completed a strategic planning process that identified challenges regarding emerging workforce needs and the contributions that BCC could make to its changing region. BCC's president, Jean Floten, conducted informational interviews with over one hundred top corporate executives, representing the Boeing Company, Microsoft Corporation, and small and medium-sized high-technology firms. These interviews documented both an extensive need for information technology (IT) workers and a growing "qualification gap" between the knowledge and skills desired by employers and new workers' actual level of preparation. The interviews also indicated that the technology workforce shortage was far more extensive than initially believed, and much greater than an individual institution could adequately address.

To support a regional response to the lack of qualified technology employees, BCC facilitated the formation of the Regional Advanced Technology Education Consortium (RATEC). This consortium is composed of ten business representatives (including the Washington Software Alliance, which represents more than 1,000 IT companies), more than forty high schools, ten community colleges, and six four-year public and private universities. RATEC's objective is to facilitate the development of improved advanced technology education among its members.

BCC then applied for and received a National Science Foundation (NSF) Advanced Technology Education Center award in 1995 to establish the North-West Center for Emerging Technologies (NWCET). NWCET's mission is to improve IT education in order to increase the supply, quality, and diversity of the IT workforce.

In addition to the development of IT curricula and degree programs, the NSF grant provides the NWCET with funding to gather, organize, and disseminate research on IT careers. Working with RATEC and IT professionals, the NWCET identified eight primary IT career clusters. This research also revealed a disparity between the actual degree level needed to perform many IT jobs and the image projected that employee shortages must be met by four-year graduates in software engineering and systems analysis. The NWCET research showed that the skills attained by two-year graduates matched six of the eight identified career clusters (NWCET, 1997). These findings indicate a strong role for community and technical colleges in filling the IT workforce shortfall.

To better define IT careers, the NWCET and the Washington Software Alliance asked companies to provide high-technology employees within the eight career clusters to participate in a collaborative process called a DACUM (Develop a Curriculum). In the DACUM process, a group of six to eight practitioners of the job under study are assembled in a panel to identify the tasks performed in that job and the skills required to perform those tasks. The NWCET DACUM panels conducted this process for each of the clusters and also identified the Secretary's Commission on Achieving Necessary Skills (SCAN) tools, knowledge, and foundation skills required to do the job well (U.S. Dept. of Labor, 1992). The results of the work were summarized in *Building a Foundation for Tomorrow: Skill Standards for Information Technology* (NWCET, 1997). This document, published with support from Boeing, the National Science Foundation, and the Washington State Board of Community and Technical Colleges, is being disseminated regionally and nationally.

This publication has been instrumental in the development of new IT programs and partnerships between educational institutions and businesses. Using the skill standards, high schools are developing a core IT curriculum; community colleges are developing and revising programs in technical support, interactive digital media, programmer/analyst, and database associate; and the University of Washington is developing a new program in computing and software systems and in management of technology-based organizations. As a result of this collaborative effort, the region now has a true 2 + 2 + 2 (high school + two-year college + baccalaureate) option for students in IT with solid industry-based data to demonstrate the economic potential for graduates.

RATEC's industry partners, along with a growing list of new partners, have agreed to keep IT industry data current and to use new and developing data for the ongoing implementation of programs that address workforce needs. RATEC serves as the primary regional mechanism to disseminate the NWCET's findings, to form new partnerships among existing members, and to identify new participants for IT-related projects. RATEC is also addressing recruitment needs by developing a marketing video directed at high school students and their parents.

Identifying and Developing High-Wage Programs

A second challenge for BCC was in identifying potential high-wage jobs in emerging technology fields and finding the resources to develop the educational and training programs needed to support these fields. Potential new programs come to the attention of college staff in various ways. CEOs inform the college president of their needs; faculty identify new job categories through research as well as contacts in the field; advisory committees provide input on market trends; NWCET research reveals changing and emerging jobs and skill sets; information is collected at conferences and from other colleges; or the vocational director may identify new jobs through targeted research, state workforce data, or contacts with colleagues or other professionals. The very speed at which new jobs in technology fields are emerging further compounds the complexity and importance of the research process. With limited resources and pressure to produce more high-wage graduates, BCC needs to make informed decisions about which job fields to pursue.

BCC's first step was to set aside two full-time faculty positions funded from growth FTE allocations (that is, state funds received by the college on the basis of its enrollment growth), and to reserve them for new high-wage programs. To decide how to allocate these new positions, the vocational director embarked on an intensive four-month research project. For each potential field, initial job availability and wage data was gathered to narrow the field to high-demand, high-wage jobs. This too, however, led to additional complications.

Determining market need and wages can be challenging in quickly emerging information technology fields. BCC found that state economic data, the source normally used to justify new programs to the state board staff who must approve them, could lag the high-technology industry by as much as three years. For example, within the past year the college had to use a consortium of businesses asking for Call Center training to convince the state system staff that Call Center jobs were indeed high-wage jobs, because the state's data did not support that picture. This and other examples forced BCC to turn once again to businesses to gather data to support its case. BCC utilized a number of business resources, including market data research, web-based research, executive and professional technician interviews, input from advisory committees, and updates from the NWCET and RATEC and professional organizations such as Global Wireless Education Consortium, the Information Technology Alliance Association, and the Washington Software Alliance. These sources are able to provide current data on several of the IT jobs being considered by BCC and its partners, including network and wireless technicians. Other job data, on fields as diverse as digital music and specialized network technician, were supplied by contacts in the businesses themselves.

The process of developing the curricula for these new, emerging fields has benefited from the work done by the NWCET and its grant partners. As mentioned earlier under partnerships, BCC looked to industry to ensure students that the skills learned would match industry-identified needs. Focusing on the industry-identified skills standards, additional industry-based DACUM's are helping BCC identify the specific skills needed in these new fields. The same business partnerships that were formed in researching the career clusters are now helping generate the course content, even before the faculty have been hired.

In the process of identifying the new programs, BCC also discovered that IT programs would require a substantial investment in new equipment. The college's resources were insufficient to meet the need. Partnerships and grants were again key to solving the problem. For the wireless technician program, BCC partnered with another area college that had already started the program and invested in equipment. BCC will offer portions of the curriculum on its campus and use the labs at the other campus for "hands-on" instruction. State workforce grants are providing startup funding for equipment for the multimedia and networking program, as well as for a revised technical support program.

As BCC moves to market these new programs, the college recognizes that recruitment may be yet another stumbling block. Potential students may know as little about these emerging fields as BCC did before beginning this project. Our interactions with parents and students in area high schools has shown that both are still heavily oriented toward four-year degrees as the optimum educational goal. As a result, students receive little encouragement to consider two-year technical degrees, despite the high earning potential of these new technological careers. The college is partnering with local private industry councils, the Washington State Employment Security Department, and community-based organizations such as Eastside Youth Services, Jewish Family Services, and others to introduce potential students to these high-wage, high-demand jobs. BCC has also partnered with Microsoft to use the Microsoft

Skills 2000 aptitude/interest inventory tool to introduce an even wider audience to the fields of information technology through web-based communication. Other tools, such as the video being developed by RATEC featuring community and technical college graduates in these new high-wage jobs, can help present a positive picture of emerging IT occupations and the career potential they offer.

Responding to State Accountability Measures

A final area in which earnings information is playing a critical role for BCC is in the performance funding indicators identified by the Washington state legislature in 1997. In this first year of implementation, one of the four indicators on which the community and technical college system was required to show progress was a workforce improvement goal: increasing the average hourly wage of professional/technical program graduates. Given BCC's focus on health and IT programs, the college was not surprised to find that its professional/technical graduates, at a median wage of $13 per hour, were already at the highest level in Washington state and exceeded the state legislative goal by $1 per hour (SBCTC, 1997). However, upward progress was the goal and BCC needed to respond.

One of the strategies chosen by BCC was to shift the enrollment balance between lower and higher wage programs by adding capacity in high-wage, high-demand IT programs while holding the capacity constant in lower-wage programs such as early childhood education and recreation leadership. During the past year, BCC dedicated part of its FTE growth to this strategy by adding sections to existing high-wage IT programs. It also committed to adding two new IT programs next year: networking and telecommunications.

As BCC worked on this state goal, college staff became aware of the need to understand the derivation of the data being supplied by the state system, and of our own data as well. For example, we discovered that the state system wage data have an approximate fifteen- to eighteen-month time lag. This meant that data we were given in the fall of 1997 were actually based on the earnings of June 1996 graduates. We needed to recognize that any changes in the wage data reported in the fall of 1998 (the end of our first year of implementation) would actually be the result of college or market changes that took place before performance funding was in place. The impact of the program changes we made this year won't be known until fall of 1999. It will be important for our staff and for those reporting these data to recognize this lag in impact.

We also discovered differences between the state's placement of our programs into high, medium, and low-wage categories and the information we had gathered locally on our graduates. For example, BCC's large administrative office systems (AOS) program is categorized by the state as a low-wage program (for 1996–1997 that meant under $8/hr), and considerably affects the college's profile of percentages of graduates in high, medium, and low-wage occupations. BCC had gathered data on June 1997 AOS graduates that placed them at a median hourly wage of $11.54, thus putting them in the high-wage program category. Admittedly there was a year's difference in the data, but it seemed too great to be the result of one year's shift in market wages. A check with state board staff on this discrepancy yielded the information that programs are placed into the high, medium, or low-wage categories based on state-wide averages, and may not be reflective of local conditions. Their own data for BCC showed a median wage of $9.75/hr for our June 1996 graduates (placing BCC's program in the medium wage category), still considerably different from our own figures.

A third measurement issue emerged in examining data for interior design graduates. Washington State Employment Security data do not include people who are self-employed or working as individual contractors. It relies on company-provided employee data. We have not surveyed our interior design graduates to establish their self-employment rate, but the program chair estimates that it may be as high as 50 percent. Those graduates are not reflected in the state profile of our program. BCC anticipates that this omission could have a significant impact on several IT programs, such as networking, software support, and multimedia design, where many graduates work as consultants or individual contractors. The state is working to find a way to obtain this information. Until then, if we are to have a full profile of the earnings of our graduates, it will be important for us to identify programs in which a high percentage of graduates are self-employed, and to gather our own earnings information.

There are several important issues in these data problems, for the college and the system. One is in how the information is reported to the public. Performance funding has a high degree of visibility with the legislature and the public. Local newspapers are very interested in the results, and are inclined to publish them with intriguing headlines such as "local college in bottom third of state." It is important for us to be able to explain data limitations. It is just as important to understand these limitations internally. We are encouraging faculty and staff to make data-based decisions as they work on a variety of BCC- and state-identified performance goals. The staff making recommendations for improvement strategies and the indicators to measure them need to understand those indicators thoroughly in order to select effective strategies and build confidence in the data. We have learned to ask a lot of questions about the state's indicators, to be careful about the data we supply to faculty and staff groups, and to think about long-term impact. BCC has also developed a close working relationship with the state board staff in order to understand how the data are gathered and to provide them feedback on the problems we discover. Together we hope to improve state-gathered data and to identify where it will be important to supplement state data with locally gathered data to provide an accurate profile of placement and earnings.

Summary

From its work over the last three years, BCC has learned the value of earnings data and the difficulty of obtaining them for rapidly emerging fields. The college now recognizes that earnings data on its graduates should be gathered locally as well as by the state to provide a full picture and as a check on the usefulness of the state data. Because the state data may lag or not reflect local conditions for BCC professional/technical programs, industry partners and industry-based professional associations will be critical to providing the earnings data needed to justify new program starts. Partnerships with businesses and other educational institutions can make it possible to enter into expensive, quickly changing technology fields that would not be economically advantageous for a single college. Partnerships may also provide more accurate profiles of employers' needs through focus groups, DACUMs, and industry-related professional groups. Finally, earnings data are important not only to satisfy accountability requirements, but also to help convince students and parents of the attractiveness of changing traditional fields and emerging occupations.

References

NorthWest Center for Emerging Technologies. *Building a Foundation for Tomorrow: Skill Standards for Information Technology.* Bellevue, Wash.: NorthWest Center for Emerging Technologies, Bellevue Community College, 1997.

State Board for Community and Technical Colleges (SBCTC). "Summary of District Accountability for Improvement Plans: State Performance Funding 1997–1998." State Board for Community and Technical Colleges Web site (http://www.sbctc@ctc.edu), Performance Funding, December 1997.

U.S. Department of Labor. *Learning a Living: A Blueprint for High Performance.* The Secretary's Commission on Achieving Necessary Skills. Washington, D.C.: U.S. Department of Labor, April, 1992.

Kae R. Hutchison is special assistant to the president for institutional effectiveness at Bellevue Community College in Bellevue, Washington.

Sharon Story Kline is director of development at Bellevue Community College in Bellevue, Washington.

Carol Mandt is director of educational projects, NorthWest Center for Emerging Technologies, Bellevue Community College, Bellevue, Washington.

Suzanne L. Marks is director of professional and technical programs at Bellevue Community College in Bellevue, Washington.

For half a decade, Southwestern College has attempted to assess its economic impact on its service area in terms of college employment and the expenditures it makes. Thanks to a new statewide information system, the college now incorporates the post-college earnings of its students as part of a larger picture of economic benefits for the community and its students. This chapter describes how state wage data are converted for local use in college planning, program improvement, and measurement of institutional effectiveness.

Institutional Level Implementation: Translating Research into Current Practice

Fred Carvell, Martha Graham, William E. Piland

Currently, Southwestern College (SWC) is the only public institution of higher education located in the 167-square-mile western and southernmost corner of the United States. The main campus is located twelve miles south of the city of San Diego and eight miles north of the international border with Mexico and the thriving city of Tijuana. The college also operates an educational center in San Ysidro, within eyesight of the border crossing.

The district population of 376,000 is highly diverse in ethnicity, age, employment patterns, and educational attainment. Over half of the residents are minorities, mostly Hispanic, along with people of Asian-Pacific and African-American descent. The cultural diversity of the population is accompanied by some challenging demographic characteristics. Compared to the county average, the number of low-income families is greater, the average educational attainment is lower, and the unemployment rate, even in good economic times, is higher. On average the college serves approximately 4.3 percent of the total adult population in its service area.

The diversity of the community is reflected in the characteristics of SWC's 16,000 students. Fifty-five percent are Hispanic, 20 percent are Asian and Pacific Islanders, and 5 percent are African American. Over half of the students are women (55 percent); the average student age is twenty-seven, with day students being younger than evening students; over 40 percent are self-supporting; and nearly half work full- or part-time while attending college. Four out of ten students want to transfer to a university, about 10 percent want an associate degree, nearly 20 percent have a career-related goal, and the rest have a variety of educational objectives, including self-improvement, or are undecided about a college major.

Measuring Economic Impact of the College

The college district is home for some 5,500 employers, most of which are small. Less than 2 percent hire over 100 workers, and 75 percent employ fewer than 10 people. SWC is the fifth largest employer in its service area.

In a community of small businesses, primarily engaged in trade, commerce, and service industries, the role of the college in the local economy is of paramount importance. In keeping with its institutional goal of contributing to the economic development of the region, Southwestern College attempts to assess its economic impact on the community. This impact includes at least three powerful factors: income generation, job creation, and credit base expansion (Piland and Erzen, 1988). These economic impacts are quantifiable and can be estimated with reasonable accuracy, as explained briefly below.

Income Generation. Total income generated by the business operations of a college is derived from three primary sources: (1) direct expenditures for goods and services purchased from local businesses, (2) the payroll of college employees and student workers, and (3) the financial assistance received by students. These direct college expenditures are supplemented by a multiplier effect. In essence, each dollar spent by a college on employee wages and local purchases becomes, in part, a dollar of income for local businesses. These businesses, in turn, spend some portion of their income with other local businesses. This *chain of expenditures* will continue through several cycles so that the income generation effect of each original dollar spent by the college is multiplied by some factor, usually in the range of 1.45 to 2.35 (Caffrey and Issacs, 1971). This becomes a significant factor, considering that the total annual budget of SWC is over $40 million dollars, of which over 80 percent is allocated to employee salaries and benefits. A 1998 study demonstrated that SWC had a total economic impact of $37 million dollars in the district during one year. This figure included a direct impact of direct district expenditures ($24.7 million) and indirect expenditures ($12 million) (Piland, 1998).

Job Creation. Colleges provide jobs, directly and indirectly, for community residents. In the case of Southwestern College, 225 academic faculty and administrators, 300 classified employees, and well over 600 student workers are employed annually. In addition, more than 400 part-time faculty are hired each year, and over 100 part-time classified personnel augment the full-time college work force. In addition to these full- and part-time college jobs, other jobs exist in the local community as a result of college business activities. This *job creation coefficient* ranges from 70 to 90 jobs per million dollars spent by the college on wages and business transactions in the area in which it is located (Ryan, 1985). The Piland and Erzen (1988) study cited earlier further demonstrated that SWC accounted for an additional 1,729 full-time jobs in the local community.

Credit Base Expansion. Financial institutions in the college service area benefit from the checking and savings deposits and investments made by the college and its employees. These funds add to the credit base of these financial institutions and enable them to engage in lending activities. Likewise, borrowers benefit from the increased availability of increased funds for business and consumer loans. Average college savings, checking account balances, and employee earnings, which factor out at between 4 and 7 percent of total employee compensation, expand the credit base in the local community (U.S. Bureau of the Census, 1996). Based on these sources, the combination of college deposits and employee savings in one fiscal year added over $7 million dollars to the community credit base (Piland, 1998).

These three quantifiable economic impact factors contribute to the economic heartbeat of the communities in which the college is located; therefore, they are used periodically to analyze its economic impact in the community. Recently, however, SWC was provided the tools to add another dimension to the measure of its economic value: the ability to calculate, with a high degree of accuracy and success, the earnings of its former students. Thanks to a new statewide management information system for computing and reporting the wage and salary earnings of former community college students, SWC has not only enlarged its capacity beyond the original concept of measuring economic impact but has also enhanced its ability to engage in more focused college planning, program review, and measuring institutional effectiveness.

College Use of Wage Data of Former Students

Local use of state wage data for former community college students involves four major steps at SWC: (1) conversion and adaptation of state data to local circumstances, (2) analysis and interpretation of wage data for former SWC students and comparison with state averages, (3) communications and dissemination of information, and (4) development of strategies for utilization of study findings.

Conversion and Adaptation of State Data. In spring 1997, SWC first received wage data from the California Community Colleges Chancellor's Office Management Information System (MIS). The report included wage information both for community college students statewide and for SWC's students whose last year in college was 1991–1992. The data were obtained by matching, where possible, students' Social Security numbers with wage records on file with the California Employment Development Department's Unemployment Insurance (EDD/UI) division. This massive statewide effort was an undertaking that no single community college could afford to do individually.

Components of the State Wage Data. State wage data were compiled for the total 1991–1992 statewide student cohort and individual community college cohorts for three time periods: last year in college (1991–1992); first year out of college (1992–1993), and third year out of college (1994–1995). Both state and SWC wage data were summarized in three ways: (1) all students were reported, regardless of major, (2) all vocational students were reported by assigned program major and by status of program completion, that is, leaver (those who did not earn a certificate or degree), certificate earners, or AA/AS holders, and (3) all vocational students were also categorized by demographic characteristics, that is, sex, ethnicity, and age group.

Local Analysis and Interpretation of Wage Data. The state provided the wage data and guidelines for use by local colleges but performed no analysis for individual colleges. The SWC Planning and Research Office compiled the state and local MIS data for use in college planning and program review. Although the statewide data were valuable to local colleges, five factors had to be considered in determining their specific applicability to SWC.

First, the median earnings of students in their final year of college had to be weighed against the fact that over half of the SWC students who work while attending college do so part-time, thus depressing the median income. As a result, it was agreed that a better gauge of the benefits of college to wage earning capabilities is the comparison between first and third year out of college earnings.

Second, the data reported the students' programs of study in which they were enrolled during their last term of college but not the occupation in which they were employed one to three years later. Whether former SWC students were employed in an occupation directly related to their vocational program in college could not be determined.

Third, although SWC data reported almost 7,000 total students who had left the college, only forty-six of those students who had earned a certificate were reported. The reason for the lack of data on certificate completers is not clear. One possible explanation is the relatively low number of certificate holders combined with their low employment rates during that recessionary period. Since the state reported no demographic or program data in instances with five or fewer cases, most of the details for the certificate students were unavailable, thus limiting the analysis of certificate data to a very broad conclusion based on totals only, rather than by specific programs in which students had earned certificates.

Fourth, the fact that the state MIS study did not include former students who were employed by the government (federal and state) or in a military service had a significant impact on the local interpretation of the data. More than one-third of the people employed in the SWC district are employed by either military or government entities; this translates into a large proportion of our former students who were not included in the study.

Finally, when comparing the earnings of SWC's students with the state as a whole, it was important to reconcile the fact that wages in San Diego County in 1994 were generally below those of California by an average of about $3,000 a year.

Communications and Dissemination of College Findings. Despite the limitations noted above, the wage data were deemed valuable for college use in institutional planning and program review, as well as in providing a vehicle to portray to the general public the value of a community college education. Ultimately, student post-college earnings will also be used as one of the outcome measures for assessing institutional effectiveness.

Key Findings for Southwestern College. Comparisons drawn between the college and the state and among the various reporting segments within the college produced statistics that underscored the value of obtaining a college education, particularly an associate degree. For instance, despite the general wage gap between San Diego County and the state, the external comparison showed that SWC vocational students earned between 81 percent and 92 percent as much as all California community college vocational students for each of the three periods measured.

An internal comparison of wage data indicated that those vocational students who earned a certificate earned slightly less than all SWC certificate holders, but those awarded an associate degree earned about 22 percent more than other SWC degree holders. Figure 7.1 shows the comparison for some groups of students who earned a degree versus those who did not. For example, when vocational students who earned an associate degree were compared to those who did not, the degree holders earned more in most categories. In particular, Hispanics and females earned twice as much; other nonwhites earned about 60 percent more; males and students over age 25 earned about 40 percent more; vocational students earned 60 percent more; and SWC students with a degree, in general, earned about 12 percent more than those without one. A key finding for SWC was that the associate degree is an important pathway to making a sustaining living wage and enhancing career progress, especially for underrepresented minorities and women.

Strategies for Utilization of Findings. By the end of the year after the state MIS first provided the data, findings from the comprehensive analysis of wage earnings of former SWC students were used by the college to (1) communicate with its staff, students, and general public about the value of completing programs of study and earning an associate degree, (2) provide a basis for developing goals and objectives for the college master plan, (3) use selected wage data to establish criteria for assessing relevant vocational-technical programs, and (4) establish an indicator of institutional effectiveness. Converting the study findings into a useful format for these purposes presented challenges of their own and called for different communications strategies.

First, the SWC planning and research office described the detailed analysis and findings in a written report that was distributed to the entire college management team (academic administrators, managers, and unit supervisors) and faculty leadership. Because this was the first time the statewide student wage data were available to the college, great efforts were made not only to convert and analyze the data for local use but also to establish procedures whereby the analysis could be institutionalized and continued annually as wage data for future student cohorts become available.

Second, to further facilitate internal and external communications, a two-page summary ("Research Notes") was produced containing key findings and

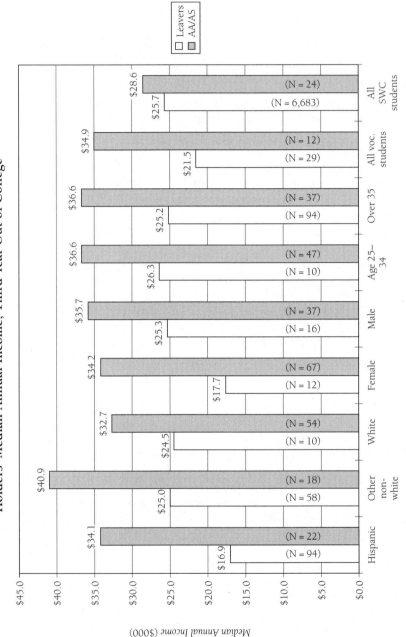

Figure 7.1. Comparison of SWC Vocational Leavers' and Vocational AA/AS Degree Holders' Median Annual Income, Third Year Out of College

their implications. The full research report was used to establish the authenticity of the findings and define the procedures for continuation of the study. The shorter "Research Notes" was used to disseminate the information widely to interested parties. Copies of "Research Notes" were distributed to all college faculty and staff. Future plans include making such information available electronically as well. The public information office used the findings to contact local news media, resulting in several feature articles in newspapers, including those directed to the Spanish-speaking community.

Third, the SWC planning and research staff made internal presentations at college staff development workshops attended by faculty, administrators, and other employees during the academic year. During these presentations, study findings were explained along with their potential usefulness for student counseling and instructional planning. These dissemination strategies raised college and community awareness about the value of completing programs and the increased earnings potential of an associate degree.

As noted earlier, the study findings had implications for two other college functions, namely, institutional planning and program review. Each of these had audiences who needed to receive the information and an explanation of how it could be used. At the time local wage data became available, a major college effort was in place to update the institutional master plan. Copies of "Research Notes" were given to the college planning team responsible for setting three-year goals. A member of the college research staff worked with this group to explain the findings and assist the goal-setting team to incorporate the information when establishing relevant three-year institutional goals and objectives.

The same strategy was used to convey the information about wage data to appropriate academic deans and faculty program review teams who assess designated college educational programs annually. About 25 percent of the some 100 instructional programs are assessed each year. The post-college wage data for each program in which SWC students had enrolled were analyzed and submitted to the relevant teams for use in assessment of program and student outcomes. In these cases, first- and third-year student earnings were used.

Another critical area in which SWC uses post-college wage data is in identifying and using measures for assessing institutional effectiveness. At SWC, this has been given high priority in the three-year plan. As a result, the college planning and research unit has been charged with designing and implementing a system for coordinating, collecting, and synthesizing information on more than twenty indicators of institutional effectiveness. Among those agreed upon measures was post-college (three-year) student earnings by ethnicity, gender, and program major. The SWC planning and research office has established and implemented a process for accessing, analyzing, and comparing SWC student post-college wage data annually and reporting the findings to the college management team and board of governors.

Conclusion

What started out to be the addition of post-college wage data to the other factors used to gauge the economic impact of the college in the community has resulted in making available valuable information for the college planning process, has added a new dimension to the assessment of career programs, and has contributed to the measurement of institutional effectiveness. These specific results, along with the general information that can be conveyed to college staff and students and the general public, show that collaborative efforts between state agencies and local colleges can be enlightening, beneficial, and cost effective.

References

Caffrey, J., and Issacs, H. "Estimating the Impact of a District or University on the Local Economy." Washington, D.C.: American Council on Education, 1971.

Piland, W. E., and Erzen, R. "Community Colleges: Major Business Enterprises with Economic Impact." *Trustee Quarterly,* Summer, 1988, 1–5.

Piland, W. E. *Southwestern College Follow-up Economic Impact Study.* San Diego, Calif.: Office of Research and Services for Postsecondary Education, College of Education, San Diego State University, 1998.

Ryan, J. "A Shortcut to Estimating Economic Impact." *Community/Junior College Quarterly,* 1985, 197–214.

U.S. Bureau of the Census. *Statistical Abstract of the United States: 1996* (115 Edition). Washington, D.C.: U.S. Bureau of the Census, 1996.

FRED CARVELL *is retired special assistant for planning and research, Southwestern College, Chula Vista, California.*

MARTHA GRAHAM *is research analyst, College Planning and Research Office, Southwestern College, Chula Vista, California.*

WILLIAM E. PILAND *is professor of education, San Diego State University.*

This chapter highlights selected results of the post-college earnings of students from California community colleges. Specifically, it presents analyses by age group, vocational major, and economic disadvantage, and discusses the methodology and policy implications of the use of earnings data derived from administrative databases.

Descriptive Analysis of Students' Post-College Earnings from California Community Colleges

Frankie Santos Laanan

With 107 community colleges, seventy-one districts, and over 1.4 million students enrolled, California's community college system is the largest system of higher education in the world. In fact, about 10 percent of all U.S. college students attend a California community college and about 20 percent of all community college students in the United States attend a California community college (National Center for Education Statistics, 1994). Further, California's enrollment of more than a million students is more than twice the enrollment of any other state (American Association of Community Colleges, 1996, p. 7). Given its "open-access" philosophy, the goal of the colleges is to provide a low-cost, high-quality postsecondary opportunity for a broad array of clients—from first-generation students to working adults and senior citizens.

Questions of the contributions that community colleges make to an individual's economic worth have been posed in terms of income enhancement. States including California (Friedlander, 1993a, 1993b), Florida (Pfeiffer, 1990), North Carolina (Vanderheyden, 1994), Texas (Froeschle, 1991), and Washington (Seppanen, 1993, 1994) have conducted statewide studies using the Employment Development Department's unemployment insurance (EDD-UI) wage record data, and have developed a methodology to measure students' post-college earnings by using these data. Most of the studies have followed program completers or graduates into the workplace to estimate average annual earnings or placement.

As in many other states, the issue of establishing accountability measures to assess students' post-college earnings received immediate attention from

California educators, vocational and occupational administrators, faculty, and legislators. An important policy question is to what extent do students benefit financially, as measured by their post-college earnings, in completing a vocational certificate or associate degree? This chapter reports the relevant statewide data on students who last attended a California community college during the 1992–1993 academic year.

California's Efforts to Study Post-College Earnings

Jack Friedlander, in conjunction with the California Community Colleges Chancellor's Office (CCCCO), pioneered the state's early efforts in this field. In a newsletter (*California Community Colleges, Administrators of Occupational Education, 1992*), Friedlander described the possible utility of the UI wage record data collected by the EDD. At that time, he solicited the support of key state policy makers and campus-based leaders to consider using UI wage record data as a method of conducting follow-up studies on the success of former occupational education program students in the labor market.

Interagency Collaboration. Before an assessment could be made about students' post-college earnings, the state chancellor's office and the California EDD had to conduct a data exchange procedure. This process involved electronically matching students' Social Security numbers (SSNs) in the UI wage record data collected and maintained by the California EDD with the demographic and educational data for all California community college students stored in the chancellor's office Management Information System (MIS). Similar to employers in most states, California employers are required to comply with UI compensation law by submitting UI quarterly reports of earnings of their employees. Additional information about the employer is also reported, such as the employer identification number, the county in which the business is located, and the industry affiliation of the business.

Research Studies. The data exchange process led to Friedlander's (1993a) feasibility study in which the coordinated efforts of the CCCCO, California EDD, and two community colleges were formalized. This feasibility study was used to develop the Post-Education Employment Tracking System (PEETS) to track the post-college employment rates and earnings of community college program completers and leavers over an extended period. Friedlander concluded that PEETS can be used not only to answer questions about employment patterns of former students, but also to provide information about employment rates by major and type of degree, comparative earnings of associate degree graduates and those who did not complete the degree, earnings and employment rates in different population groups, and a few other outcomes.

To refine the use of PEETS, Friedlander (1996) conducted a follow-up study that included a sample of 173,523 students from eighteen California community colleges. The results of the study revealed the following: UI records were available for the majority of the sample; wages of students who received a certificate or degree from an occupational program were higher than both those who left occupational programs without a degree or certificate and those who completed nonoccupational programs; occupational students with a degree or certificate experienced a 47 percent gain in wage between their last year of college and third year after college; PEETS is an inexpensive method for tracking the success of former students; and the information can be used to meet accreditation requirements to respond to consumer inquiries.

Methodology and Data Sources

The reporting domain of the cohort includes students with a Social Security number who met the full term reporting criteria and were enrolled in at least a half unit or eight hours of positive attendance during the academic year. The SSN serves as the universal identifier that is unique to all students.

A unique aspect of California's studies of students' post-college earnings is the categorization of students. Other states have collected data on students who completed only vocational programs. The MIS has developed two broad categories: completers and leavers. A *completer* is a student who received a certificate or associate degree, whereas a *leaver* is a student who did not receive a certificate or associate degree but may have completed some units. For students in the leaver category, analysis could be conducted by the number of units completed. For example, data are aggregated in the following educational attainment categories: noncredit or 0 units, 0.01–11.99 units, 12–23.99 units, 24+ units, certificates, and AA or AS degree.

Exclusions from Data File. Important to note are those individuals who are excluded from the reporting domain. Students who were concurrently enrolled in K–12 during the cohort year, enrolled in any California State University (CSU) during the two years following the cohort year, and enrolled in one year following the end of the cohort year at any community college in the California community college system were excluded. Students who were employed by the military or federal government (for example, U.S. Postal Service), self-employed, unemployed, or not in the workforce were also excluded from the data set. Acknowledgment of these limitations is critical when making interpretations about the data.

Adjustment of Earnings. The median annual earnings reported in this chapter have been adjusted for inflation with the Consumer Price Index (CPI). This procedure is critical to make any real comparisons of earnings from last year in college, to first year out of college, and up to third year out of college. For the purposes of this study, all earnings were adjusted to 1996 dollars. The chancellor's office decided to use the median annual earnings instead of the average earnings because the median is a more stable statistic and not influenced by extreme outliers. The annual earnings are derived by summing earnings for those working all four quarters.

Statewide Results

There were 765,533 *leavers* and *completers* during the 1992–93 academic year. Of these students, 64,969 (or 8.5 percent) were found to have continued at one of the twenty-three California State University (CSU) campuses, and of these, over 7,900 (or 12.2 percent) had completed an associate degree or certificate at a community college. After removing these students from the database, the final adjusted sample consisted of 700,564 students. Students under twenty-five were 32.5 percent (n = 227,443) of the cohort; students twenty-five and over were 67.5 percent (n = 473,121). About five percent (n = 37,044) of all leavers and completers were identified as vocational students. These are students who successfully completed twelve or more units of vocational course work in a single program area. It is important to note that the students in the *vocational major* category were not self-identified but were ascertained from course-taking patterns assessed by the MIS office.

Table 8.1 illustrates the percentage change in median annual earnings of students by age group and educational attainment level. Specifically, the table reports the percentage change in median annual earnings from students' last year in college to third year out of college. The data compare students who are under twenty-five with those twenty-five and over. For students under twenty-five, the greatest change three years out is among certificate completers (+101.4 percent). In addition to experiencing the largest percentage gain, certificate completers also had the highest median annual earnings ($22,539). The second largest gain in median annual earnings was among students who completed the associate degree (+100.4 percent). Essentially, the findings for younger students support the notion that there is a strong positive relationship between percentage gains and educational attainment.

For older students, the pattern is similar; however, the magnitude of the percentage gains is substantially lower. For example, the gains among certificate and associate degree completers are 18.5 percent and 34.7 percent, compared with 101.4 percent and 100.4 percent for younger students. The results suggest that for older students, completing the associate degree and certificate are positively related to higher gains three years out. Yet the differences between the two levels are not substantial. A plausible explanation for the differences in percentage gains between younger and older students is that older students were making higher wages when they initially attended college. The data clearly show the disparity between younger and older students' median earnings. With years of experience under their belt, it is likely that older students will experience post-college gains but not as exaggerated. The findings do, however, support the notion that there is a positive relationship between gains and educational attainment level, regardless of age.

Table 8.2 shows the match rate and earnings of students by selected major field. The data reflect information for *all students* in the respective field, including all educational attainment levels. Specifically, the percentage of students who were found working four quarters during the first year out of college and

Table 8.1. Percentage Change in Median Annual Earnings of Students from California Community Colleges in 1992–1993 Academic Year by Age Group and Educational Attainment Level (1996 Dollars)

| | Age Group | | | | | |
| | Students Under 25 (n =227,443) | | | Students 25 and Over (n = 473,121) | | |
Educational Attainment Level	Last Year in College	Third Year Out of College	Percentage Change	Last Year in College	Third Year Out of College	Percentage Change
All students	$11,403	$18,075	58.5	$28,587	$30,505	6.7
Associate degree	9,985	20,007	100.4	24,064	32,408	34.7
Certificate	11,190	22,539	101.4	25,893	30,684	18.5
24+ units	11,243	19,157	70.4	27,449	30,118	9.7
12–23.99 units	11,112	18,198	63.8	28,693	30,483	6.2

*Excluded from this table are students in the noncredit or 0 units and 0.01–11.99 units categories.

Source: California Community Colleges Chancellor's Office, Management Information System (1997).

Table 8.2. Match Rate and Earnings by Selected Major Field: Leavers and Completers from California Community Colleges in 1992–1993 Academic Year

Major Field	First Year Out of College		Third Year Out of College	
	Percent Worked Four Quarters	Earnings	Percent Worked Four Quarters	Earnings
Aeronautical and aviation technology	68	$24,063 (06)	69	$29,627 (05)
Automotive technology	65	18,295 (09)	64	22,455 (09)
Business management	70	25,986 (05)	63	28,439 (06)
Computer and information science, general	68	29,724 (02)	69	36,503 (01)
Dental technician	74	20,671 (07)	79	25,069 (08)
Drafting technology	62	19,943 (08)	61	26,913 (07)
Electronics and electric technology	72	27,300 (04)	69	33,226 (04)
Graphic arts	66	13,371 (10)	62	18,677 (10)
Nursing	74	29,540 (03)	65	35,523 (02)
Radiological technology	82	33,435 (01)	58	34,976 (03)

The number in parentheses represents the field's ranking within each period.
Source: California Community Colleges Chancellor's Office, Management Information System (1997).

third year out is reported, along with their median annual earnings. According to the results, several technical fields (aeronautics, computers, and electronics) and radiology, business, and nursing had the highest earnings first year out. A similar pattern is found three years out.

Figure 8.1 depicts the percentage change in median annual earnings of economically disadvantaged students ($n = 4,925$) from California community colleges by educational attainment level in the 1992–1993 academic year. Identified as vocational students, these students completed a minimum of twelve units in the same program area. To be in this category, students had to have met one of the following criteria: (1) awarded a Board of Governor's grant, (2) awarded a Pell grant, (3) identified as a Greater Avenue for Independence (GAIN) participant, or (4) identified as a participant in the Job Training Partnership Program (JTPA).

The bar chart shows the percentage change for three periods: last year in college to first year out of college, last year in college to third year out of college, and first year out of college to third year out of college. This analysis illustrates the changes and the extent to which they differ for the respective periods and illustrates the magnitude of the change for each analytic period.

Last year in college to first year out of college. The results in Figure 8.1 show that the changes from students' last year in college earnings to first year out

Figure 8.1. Percentage Change in Median Annual Earnings of Economically Disadvantaged Students from California Community Colleges in 1992–1993 Academic Year by Educational Attainment Level ($n = 4,925$)

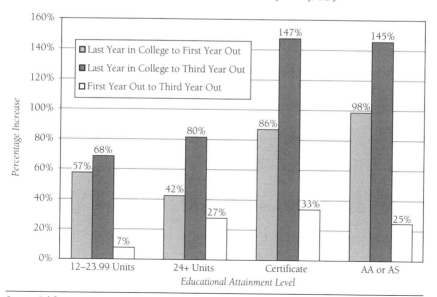

Source: California Community Colleges Chancellor's Office, Management Information System (1997).

were positive across all educational attainment levels. However, students who completed the associate degree (+98 percent) and certificate (+86 percent) realized the highest gains one year out of college. In other words, the completion of formalized programs, namely the associate and certificate, has a strong positive relationship to gains one year out.

Last year in college to third year out of college. The percentage gains over this period are substantially higher compared to the other two analyses. For example, economically disadvantaged students who complete the certificate experienced a 147 percent gain, whereas the associate degree completers experienced a 145 percent gain. A possible explanation for these extremely large gains is that students' last year in college earnings are likely to be suppressed because the students are not available to the workforce on a full-time basis at that time.

First year out of college to third year out of college. From first year out of college to third year out, economically disadvantaged students experienced positive gains across all education attainment levels. The gains range from a low of 7 percent to a high of 33 percent. Interestingly, the gains over this period are substantially smaller than for the previous one (that is, last year in college to third year out). Again, a plausible explanation is that during the last year in college, students are likely to be enrolled in courses on a part- or full-time basis and therefore are unlikely to be working full-time, Thus they are experiencing depressed wages. Analyzing first year to third year out may therefore be more realistic in terms of gauging students' post-college earnings. In conducting a "within group" analysis, students who completed the certificate experienced a 33 percent gain, followed by those completing 24+ units (27 percent), and associate degree completers (25 percent). The results suggest that for economically disadvantaged students there is a positive relationship between educational attainment and percentage gains in annual earnings three years out.

Discussion and Conclusions

The most recent findings about students from California community colleges presented here are similar to those of an earlier study conducted by Sanchez and Laanan (1997) analyzing a previous cohort. The matching procedure with EDD and the MIS data demonstrates that this strategy continues to be a cost-effective mechanism to collect and analyze students' post-college earnings.

The data suggest that compared to older students, younger students are more likely to experience greater gains between last year in college and third year out. However, older students' median annual earnings three years out are higher. As indicated earlier, a plausible explanation is that younger students may not be working full-time during their final year of college. Therefore, even though they are not earning as much as their older counterparts three years out of college, their percentage gained is greater. Among older students, completing a formalized program is positively related to gains three years out. The data reported, however, do not exclude individuals who already possess a bachelor's degree. Further analysis that controls for prior educational attainment is needed.

The data for selected majors provide descriptive information that could be useful for students as well as faculty and vocational/occupational administrators. As Grubb (1996) found, the results of this study show that fields with high median annual earnings include technical, nursing, and computer. The patterns found three years out are similar. The descriptive information suggests that major fields that require more technical training and education are likely to have higher salaries than fields that are less technical. Many of the programs listed in Table 8.2 are closely linked to business and industry. Students who complete certificate programs or associate degrees in these areas have an advantage in making the transition from school to work.

In California, as in many other states, educational institutions have developed short-term programs geared toward assisting individuals from disadvantaged backgrounds make the transition from welfare to work. These programs are prevalent in two-year institutions and adult education programs and are short-term. The findings here for economically disadvantaged students who are identified as vocational students suggest that completing formalized programs (that is, certificate or associate degree) is positively related to percentage gains in median annual earnings. This trend is evident for all three analytic periods (that is, last year to first year out, last year to third year out, and first year to third year out). Are short-term programs advantageous for this population? Are these programs assisting individuals who are attempting to make the transition from welfare to work or from unemployment to work? Critics would argue that short-term programs could do a disservice to individuals from disadvantaged backgrounds because these programs do not socialize students to the learning process or provide professional development. In other words, there is something to be said about the relationship between length of schooling and students' professional development. According to the socialization hypothesis (Pascarella and Terenzini, 1991), individuals who complete formalized degrees (for example, the baccalaureate) earn more than high school graduates because they develop skills and personal traits that make them more productive employees. Although this argument has been widely applied to four-year college graduates, the same notion could be applied to students at the community college level. Therefore, the assumption would be that students who complete an associate degree or certificate would be likely to develop highly specialized skills by virtue of completing more education compared with students who just take a few units.

In conclusion, the results presented here support earlier findings that a community college education yields gains in students' post-college earnings. More specifically, completing formalized programs, such as a certificate or associate degree, is positively related to percentage gains in annual earnings three years out. The community college system plays an integral role in providing affordable education to students with different needs. Further research needs to be conducted to examine the effects of short-term programs geared to serving special populations.

Implications for Practice

The employment and earnings information available can be used in strategic ways. Vocational/occupational deans in community colleges can examine trends data to begin to understand the earning patterns of students, both at the statewide and institutional levels.

The aggregate data currently made available to colleges must be interpreted with caution. Factors to consider include industry- or job-specific characteristics. For example, in cosmetology most individuals are self-contractors and therefore not included in the UI wage record file. Employers' needs, certificate requirements, and educational stipulations further complicate the interpretation of UI wage data. Developing a dictionary of occupations and related contextual information would assist administrators, faculty, institutional researchers, and other college personnel in interpreting these data.

Information should be filtered down to counselors and other college personnel who work closely with students. Students can benefit from obtaining labor market information as it relates to programs they are interested in pursuing. The more information students have, the better prepared they will be to make informed decisions about their educational and employment plans.

In using earnings data as a performance measure for accountability purposes, caution is required. The data currently available only provide descriptive information and, therefore, no causal inferences can be made. That is, it is impossible with the aggregate data to determine the link between students' educational training and actual employment. A more detailed follow-up study will have to be conducted to account for this relationship. Legislators, educators, policy makers, and researchers need to be aware of the methodological limitations in using administrative databases to derive performance measures. Several states have already implemented performance-based funding. Before other states begin to develop measures for accountability purposes, many variables still need to be considered.

The notion of *relatedness* of educational training and employment needs further exploration. Critics of establishing relatedness argue that it is too difficult and unnecessary to measure. Legislators who are interested in measuring a very specific outcome tend to support it. We need to ask ourselves, What is the value of measuring relatedness and what are we not gaining if we forego this process?

Colleges in California are asked to compare their data at the college or program level to the statewide data. Such comparisons raise many questions about making meaningful inferences or generalizations. Because of different economic conditions throughout the state, comparative analyses can be misleading. Incorporating information about local economic influences is important.

References

American Association of Community Colleges. *The 1996–97 AACC Annual. A State-by-State Analysis of Community College Trends and Statistics.* Washington, D.C.: American Association of Community Colleges, 1996.

California Community Colleges Administrators of Occupational Education. *CCCAOE Newsletter.* Spring, 1992.

Friedlander, J. *Using Wage Record Data to Track the Post-College Employment and Earnings of Community College Students.* Santa Barbara, Calif.: Santa Barbara City College, 1993a. (ED 360 007)

Friedlander, J. *Post-College Employment Rates and Earnings of Students Who Participated in SBCC Occupational Education Programs.* Santa Barbara, Calif.: Santa Barbara City College, 1993b. (ED 361 022)

Friedlander, J. *Using Wage Record Data to Track the Post-College Employment Rates and Wages of California Community College Students.* Santa Barbara, Calif.: Santa Barbara City College, 1996. (ED 390 507)

Froeschle, R. Pilot Study Findings of the Use of the Texas Employment Commission Unemployment Insurance Wage Records to Document Outcomes of Technical-Vocational Education and Training. Austin: Texas Higher Education Coordinating Board, 1991.

Grubb, W. N. *Working in the Middle: Strengthening Education and Training for the Mid-Skilled Labor Force.* San Francisco: Jossey-Bass, 1996.

National Center for Education Statistics. *Digest of Education Statistics, 1994.* Washington, D.C.: Government Printing Office, 1994.

Pascarella, E., and Terenzini, P. *How College Affects Students.* San Francisco: Jossey Bass, 1991.

Pfeiffer, J. J. *Florida Education and Training Placement Program.* Annual Report. Tallahassee: Florida Department of Education, 1990.

Sanchez, J. R., and Laanan, F. S. "The Economic Returns of a Community College Education." *Community College Review,* 1997, *23* (4), 73–87.

Seppanen, L. J. *Using Administrative Data Matches for Follow-Up.* Technical Report No. 93–5. Olympia: Washington State Board for Community and Technical Colleges, 1993. (ED 382 250)

Seppanen, L. J. *Job Placement Rates for Graduates of Washington Community and Technical College Vocational Programs.* Research Report No. 94–7. Olympia: Washington State Board for Community and Technical Colleges, 1994. (ED 382 255)

Vanderheyden, B. *Employment of Community College Completers.* Research Brief No. 1994–01. Raleigh: North Carolina State Department of Community Colleges, 1994. (ED 375 896)

FRANKIE SANTOS LAANAN *is senior research analyst in vocational education and institutional research at the Coast Community College District in Costa Mesa, California.*

Is a national definition to measure students' post-college/training warranted? This chapter presents policy and methodological concerns and discusses recommendations.

Looking Ahead: A National Measure of Post–Community College Earnings

Jorge R. Sanchez

In *Wealth of Nations*, Adam Smith (1776) expressed the notion that an *educated worker* could be likened to an expensive machine and that skills embodied in such a person can be "rented out" to employers. The higher the level of skills a person has, the higher this "rent" is likely to be. At first glance this metaphor seems to project little more than the harsh realities of the world of mechanized work. However, this observation helps clarify that the expected returns on investment in education is a higher level of earnings. How much return can those who attend community college expect for increasing their skills? Do the observations of yesteryear still hold true for our nation's community college student today? Are we able to conclude, on a national scale, that skills and knowledge gained at a community college increase this "rent"? Are such findings common for our nation's community colleges? Addressing the feasibility of answering these questions at a national level is the quest of this chapter.

Common Need: National Regulations

Since 1990, states have been involved in implementing the Carl D. Perkins Vocational Applied Technology Education Act (VATEA). One of the more significant elements of VATEA is its emphasis on using systematic outcome data as a program improvement device for vocational programs. VATEA established the use of measures and standards to improve occupational programs; however, it did not provide descriptions of the following terms: *outcome, measure,* or *standard.* One reason the implementation of federal mandates such as VATEA has so challenged the states is that the vision embodied in the guidelines exceeds the capacity of existing measurement tools.

Stecher and others (1995) proposed the following set of definitions for clarification in their review of VATEA: *outcome,* a measurable characteristic of student or program performance; *measure*, a method of quantifying performance in an outcome area; *standard*, the desired level of attainment or progress on a measure. Their proposal brought together a greater, uniform application of the federal policy across states; however, no mention was made regarding the development of national benchmarks or targets of performance for vocational programs. No intent was made in VATEA that the units of analysis would be national. Rather, local control, program diagnostics, improvement, and performance were clearly the intent of the legislation.

Recently, under contract to the Office of Vocational and Adult Education, U.S. Department of Education, senior researchers Klein and Medrich (1997) proposed a nationally unified approach to vocational performance measurement. Their report, *Toward Establishing a Unified System of Performance Measures*, examined the critical issue of developing uniform criteria for (1) defining vocational performance measures, (2) examining measurement populations, and (3) obtaining national aggregations of vocational education performance data.

Klein and Medrich described a framework for establishing a unified performance measurement system and a process for achieving consensus among states on a set of core measures. They contend that building consensus around a core set of national measures will probably require a clear set of federal guidelines that, at a minimum, define a set of acceptable measurement criteria and a comparable study population from which data are collected. Currently no such guidelines exist.

Anderberg and Pfeiffer (1998) suggested that the unemployment insurance (UI) wage record apparatus in each state could form the core database in developing a national or regional post-college/training follow-up system. This systematic data gathering entity could facilitate a keen understanding of the content strengths and limitations of this kind of analysis. They contend that the strength of using UI wage records is that the database represents a near-universe of wage and salary information, and that post-college/training earning analysis would provide useful vocational program performance information. To develop vocation program measures, individual student records are electronically matched to administrative employment wage records. The merged database has the capacity to generate both vocational program measures of post-college performance and individual student outcome data.

Anderberg and Pfeiffer's (1998) aim is the development of student outcome and program performance measures with state, regional, and even national scope. They proposed a means by which the data gathered from administrative and educational records can be used to describe, estimate, and analyze characteristics of groups of students and the average outcomes they achieve without regard to the identities of individuals within the study sample. Essentially, Anderberg and Pfeiffer contend that a vocational program performance measure can be attained through the aggregation of individualized student outcome measures. In this approach, program performance is the byproduct of individual post-college outcomes.

Stevens and Shi (1996) presented a brief but thorough introduction to three decades of research that has been conducted using basic administrative records for better understanding post-training/education earnings history of former vocational education students. In their guide, they sought to educate local and state authorities seeking to better understand the performance of their vocational education programs. Stevens and Shi term the use of earnings analysis "management diagnostics." They focus on earnings analysis as a vehicle for vocational educators to manage their business of voluntary behind-the-scenes diagnostics to improve their programs. Their efforts are designed to integrate post-college earnings analysis into the culture of programmatic review and enhancement rather than governmental compliance reporting, where it seems to be currently. However, many states have been too eager to rely on a single outcome measure as an absolute to justify programmatic performance funding. The jury seems to be out as to the reliability and validity of these measures across vocational programs. Nonetheless, Stevens and Shi (1996) submit that the data available in most state's UI compensation systems are similar enough to generate common post-college/training economic benefit measures.

Post-College Earnings Analysis: National Research Findings

Several prevalent research efforts (Grubb and Bragg, 1997; Stevens and others, 1992; Stevens and Shi, 1996) have reported that much of the evidence about economic gains experienced by former community college students comes from national survey and census data sets. This information compared the outcomes of large cohorts of former higher education, vocational certificate, and associate degree completers to high school students who did not attend either college or adult vocational training programs.

Specifically, Grubb and Bragg reported that "based on several different national data sets, research studies have clarified that the economic benefits of completing associate degrees and certificates are significant. Of course, these benefits are not as large as the benefits of baccalaureate degrees, [which] take two to four times as long, but [are] substantial nonetheless, especially in some fields of study (business, technical fields for men, health occupations for women). Furthermore, the benefits are highest for those in occupational fields who find jobs related to their areas of study. In addition, transfer rates to four-year colleges are now as high from occupational subjects (like business, computers, and health fields) as they are from academic subjects. Therefore, occupational programs are not by any means 'dead end' programs" (Grubb and Bragg, 1997, p. 5).

Results from several studies reviewed by Sanchez and Laanan (1997) revealed that local findings of post-college earnings analysis closely resemble national findings: students completing a vocational credential, that is, certificate or associate degree, particularly in certain fields, fare better both in short-term earnings gains and in long-term sustainable economic gains. Local research efforts have promoted the development of data for individual colleges by using UI wage records so that individual colleges can see which of their programs are more and less effective (Friedlander, 1996).

Individual colleges, however, are more interested in programmatic level measures for management diagnostics purposes. Through the use of UI earnings/wage records analysis, colleges can examine how former students from certain vocational programs are doing in the marketplace. It seems too early for such measures and methods of analysis to be practiced widely, yet this current wave of interest in post-college/training analysis and reauthorization of VATEA accentuates these important issues.

In order for post-college earnings analysis, generated from administrative records, to be of interest to community colleges, the unit of analysis must reach the program. Information about post-college earnings gains for the college in the "college-wide" aggregate form holds little value for a particular vocational program. Post-college earnings analysis relative to completion of a certificate or associate degree in a specific vocational area has more impact on students, faculty, and the public than a gross national performance measure. However, without the national measure as a tool to inform and influence the budgetary process, there may not be funds to operate or enhance local vocational programs.

To establish a national measure of post-college earnings from automated administrative records such as UI records, several key steps must occur. Anderberg and Pfeiffer (1998) have outlined some important conditions and consideration for establishing wider usage of UI-based student outcomes analysis. They emphasize that it is important to include all affected state and national agencies in this process. Agencies that administer data sets that will be tapped as sources of the outcome information are typically not involved in post-college outcomes research. State and national agencies usually do not come in contact with educational research interests. This unfamiliarity with operational and research issues can result in the development of regulations protecting individual record data from public disclosure. In addition, the establishment of written procedures to spell out the research entities' obligations with the cooperating agencies needs to be developed.

Addressing National Measurement Efforts

The amendments to the 1990 VATEA entailed major changes in federal vocational education priorities and practices. Among the most visible innovations was the creation of statewide systems of measurement and standards of performance. The purpose of these systems was to create an objective, outcome-based framework for program evaluation that could be used as the cornerstone for local program improvement. It is from these statewide systems that a national post-college/training earnings measure could emerge, although this was not the intent of VATEA.

The technology to measure vocational/occupation performance through post-college/training earnings in a reliable, valid, and efficient manner has not been widely used in many states. Although much work has been done by a few states to develop performance measures of occupational skills, this is an emerging assessment area with few operational systems in place. Some researchers contend that most states are not fully equipped to develop tools for measuring occupational outcomes. Others feel that the states are closer now than ever before to developing collaborative data exchanges similar to systems in California, Florida, and Washington.

Arriving at a uniform and consistent definition for measuring the economic benefits of attending a community college appears to be warranted. The challenges faced by state community college systems include methodological and philosophical concerns. In addition, community colleges need to develop a regional collaboration with federal and state employment agencies, the Federal Office of Manpower, Military Office of Personnel and Enlistment, United States Postal Service Office of Personnel, and neighboring states. These collaborations are required to gain control of the data matching and measurement process.

In Pursuit of a National Measure of Post-College Earnings

Not that long ago, the "new accountability" movement was based on returns on investment. The post-college earnings analysis is a return to this paradigm. In the current era there are several important considerations that colleges and vocational programs need to keep in mind when developing a national or regional post-college earnings outcome. First, they need to remember that any changes in pre- or post-earnings are a result of many factors. To attribute all the change in post-college earnings to a single variable is highly suspect. All too often changes on pre- and post-earnings are reported as a percentage increase in earnings over time. This seems simple enough; however, the adjustments must be made to convert earnings to constant dollars before percentage change is calculated. Also, adjusting for the cost of inflation in a particular economic region may be warranted.

In developing national program performance and student outcome measures, additional questions can arise. For example: (1) What types of earnings can students expect over their life-time should they complete a particular course of study at a community college? (2) Are there significant regional and state differences in earnings for a given group of occupations or program completers? (3) Are there significant college-specific or program-specific differences in post-college earnings? (4) Are there differences in the post-college earnings of groups of students within a program?

We know that over three decades, several authors, using differing methodologies, have arrived at similar results: (1) Generally, program completers, that is, graduates with a certificate or AA degree, economically outperform comparison groups based on sex and age for persons with only a high school diploma; (2) the longer the post-college completer is in the workforce, the greater the post-college earnings difference; (3) the longer the completers' program, the higher the post-college earnings; (4) certain vocational programs provide a higher post-college earnings potential than others; and (5) students who completed a community college program are less likely to be unemployed.

There is ample research comparing earnings of baccalaureate and advanced degree holders with high school graduates, whereas precious little is known of the economic benefits of a certificate or an associate degree in the world of work. Clearly, the time has come for community colleges to work collaboratively with state and national agencies to create a consortium to develop national post-community college earnings measures and student outcomes.

References

Anderberg, M., and Pfeiffer, J. J. A Field Guide to Automated Follow-up. Washington, D.C.: U.S. Department of Labor, Employment and Training Administration, 1998.

Friedlander, J. Using Wage Record Data to Track the Post-College Employment Rates and Wages of Community College Students. Santa Barbara, Calif.: Santa Barbara City College, 1996. (ED 390 507)

Grubb, W. N., and Bragg, D. "Making Connections in Times of Change." CenterWork, 1997, 8 (4).

Klein, S., and Medrich, E. Toward Establishing a Unified System of Performance Measures. U.S. Department of Education, Office of Vocational and Adult Education. Berkeley, Calif.: MPR Associates, Inc. 1997.

Sanchez, J. R., and Laanan, F. S. What Is It Worth? The Economic Value of an Associate Degree from California Community Colleges. Report Number 97–07–29–001. Costa Mesa, Calif.: Coast Community College District, 1997. (ED 413 941)

Smith, A. An Inquiry into the Nature and Cause of Wealth of Nations. London: W. Strahan and T. Cadell, 1776.

Stecher, B., Hanser, L., Rahn, M., Levesque, K., Hoachlanderz, E. G., Emanuel, D., and Klein, S. Improving Perkins II Performance Measures and Standards. Berkeley, Calif.: National Center for Research in Vocational Education, 1995.

Stevens, D. W., Richmond, P. A., Haenn, J. F., and Michie, J. S. Measuring Employment Outcomes Using Unemployment Insurance Wage Records. Washington, D.C.: Research and Evaluation Associates, Inc. 1992.

Stevens, D. W., and Shi, J. New Perspectives on Documenting Employment and Earnings Outcomes in Vocational Education. Berkeley, Calif.: National Center for Research in Vocational Education, 1996.

JORGE R. SANCHEZ is director of vocational education and institutional research at Coast Community College District in Costa Mesa, California, and doctoral candidate in higher education at the University of California, Los Angeles.

Linked administrative records offer practical opportunities to conduct management diagnostics tailored to state and local needs. State and local community college management teams should integrate and modify components drawn from current reporting systems, such as those described in other chapters of this volume. Refinements are proposed here to improve internal and external accountability.

Employment and Earnings Outcomes: New Perspectives

David W. Stevens

The Workforce Investment Act of 1998 and the anticipated Carl D. Perkins Vocational and Applied Technology Education Act Amendments will encourage states to require accountability for community college employment and earnings outcomes. Other chapters in this volume describe information systems that were designed by state and local innovators to achieve this accountability. The success of these voluntary initiatives nurtured the national response.

Pfeiffer warns in Chapter Two that success in answering accountability questions can bring unforeseen problems. Community college exposure to these pitfalls can be limited by adopting the refinements in information systems that are described here.

Community college executives are urged to think in terms of two tiers of accountability reporting. The first tier responds to external reporting requirements, and the second is for use in internal management diagnostics. Given the evolving nature of federal and state mandates, the basic specifications for Tier 1 reporting cannot be controlled by institutions. Conversely, the locus of control for Tier 2 reporting clearly resides within the institutions, although management teams will be limited to using data elements found in Tier 1 components of the information system. This chapter focuses on Tier 2 issues because this is where the opportunity lies to utilize administrative records effectively.

Incentives to Act Now

Most states that have not already invested in administrative record linkage initiatives, such as those described in this volume, will soon do so. The incentive for these actions appears in the new federal legislation. Funds are earmarked for allocation to the states based on performance rankings. Relative employment and earnings performance will be rewarded, and states will be eligible for continuous improvement bonuses. Local authorities will not be insulated from these competitive forces. States will define local performance expectations as part of an overall strategic plan to receive some of these funds.

Federal specification of the employment and earnings components will include design features described elsewhere in this volume. When states then exercise their discretionary authority to negotiate definitions of performance measures with federal counterparts, they will look to the pioneering states for guidance.

This chapter assumes that information systems used to respond to external requirements (that is, Tier 1) will include or have routine linked access to two data sources: student records documenting enrollment in selected curricula and achievement levels at exit, and employee records documenting quarterly earnings reported to a state's employment security agency to comply with the state unemployment insurance law. The simplicity of this pairing of student and employee records at the Tier 1 level belies serious interpretive challenges. Conversely, the complexity of internal management diagnostics at the Tier 2 level poses critical issues that still need to be addressed. Community college management teams equipped with information systems capable of gathering and analyzing additional performance measures will play a key role in the accountability process.

Mandated Tier 1 performance measures tend to be quite simplistic. Only two workforce measures are expected—job entry and earnings. These measures are likely to be defined so a one-time link between a former student's school data and a single quarter of state employment security agency administrative records will suffice.

Momentum is building to provide public access to selected aggregations of the paired job entry and earnings measures. Community college management teams are likely to find their career education programs defined by just two figures—the percentage of all former enrollees in designated curricula who were reported as employed during a reference quarter soon after leaving school, and the amount of documented earnings during these three months. Public release of job entry and earnings figures by selected curricula will foster uncontrollable (and potentially unfavorable) oversight and funding actions when complementary Tier 2 data have not been collected, analyzed, and prepared for timely release in easily understood formats.

The case for investing in Tier 2 information system components begins with a premise that a student record within a single community college can be linked with an employment security agency's unemployment insurance (UI) wage record file. This premise is false in some states today, but states' inability or unwillingness to carry out this link is declining. The new federal legislation will hasten this decline, but process hurdles will remain.

Seppanen makes a strong case in Chapter Three of this volume for state management of the data linkage process. Pfeiffer concurs in Chapter Two. The basic point is that public education records and state employment security agency data are confidential and subject to different laws and regulations. No state employment security agency offers each community college independent access to its administrative records. When the new federal legislative mandates filter down to the state and local levels, an all-inclusive approach to Tier 1 information system design will be encouraged. Eligibility for performance bonuses will be the enticement for uniform statewide participation.

A practical working assumption for most community college management teams should be that their state will invest in securing only enough Tier 1 information to satisfy federal reporting requirements and their state's own reporting priorities. Such limited information will not provide the data needed to answer basic accountability questions that the media will pose. Institutions that remain passive in the face of this threat will regret their inaction. Therefore, state and local authorities need to assume responsibility for specifying adequate Tier 2 requirements. Herein lies the window of opportunity described in the remainder of this chapter.

Opportunities

Community colleges do not exist in a vacuum. Each is part of a network of complementary sources of education and skill enhancement. These include high schools, public and private colleges and universities, for-profit vendors, on-the-job learning opportunities, and an exploding number of Internet sites that offer on-demand access to new skills.

Tier 2 measurement ambitions should be modest in this complex learning environment. Role-playing is an effective tool for determining appropriate measures. Work backward from questions that might be posed by oversight board members or media representatives to the data that are needed to prepare clear answers. The intensity and variety of such questions will increase when mandated accountability information is released. These questions will concentrate on what a reference program's students were doing during three periods: before enrolling, concurrently with enrollment, and after leaving but before the snapshot documentation of status.

Imagine that a template with cutout windows has been placed over the continuum of before, during, and after statuses described in the previous paragraph. The Tier 1 reporting specification might have only two windows—status upon leaving the reference curriculum and status soon thereafter. Additional windows should be added for Tier 2 diagnostics.

Seppanen's chapter describes a pre-enrollment window that supports the calculation of an earnings gain measure for former students who had some earnings in both the base period and end period. Although this is an adequate beginning, Pfeiffer's warning of pitfalls comes into play here. Change measures based on single recordings of denominator and numerator values are likely to be challenged. Management teams can expect to be asked why they selected this time interval rather than some other one. Specifically, they will be asked whether they know the effect on this ratio of a change in the base period and time interval specifications.

Seize the opportunity to promote controlled access to a continuous series of employment and earnings snapshots that can be aligned with discrete episodes of enrollment in reference curricula. These data are likely to exist already in Tier 1 information system components. Federal and state accountability mandates will specify a fixed length snapshot interval, such as the third full quarter following reference program exit. Some students exit from many curricula throughout a calendar year, so all four quarters of employment and earnings data will be retained for required reporting.

Advocate investment in better use of existing administrative records before lobbying for collecting new data elements through these sources. Each quarterly report submitted by, or on behalf of, an employer who is covered by a state's unemployment insurance law contains three common data elements—an employee's Social Security number, the reporting employer's state UI tax account number, and the amount of earnings paid to that person by the reporting employer during the reference quarter. The potential value of these data elements will not be realized through Tier 1 reporting requirements alone because mandated specifications must remain simple, for two reasons—to limit the reporting burden and cost, and to improve public understanding. Local oversight board members and media representatives will be more demanding, and potential students deserve additional information as well.

The state UI tax account number assigned to each covered employer can be used to take a first giant step toward refinement of the job entry concept that is likely to be mandated for federal accountability purposes. Begin with a denominator value defined as all terminees from the reference curriculum during a chosen base period, and with a numerator value specified as an unduplicated count of the terminees who appear in a subsequent single snapshot of reported quarterly earnings. Extract each of the numerator's pairings of an employee Social Security number and an employer state UI tax account number. Link these pairings to an earlier reference period's earnings reports chosen to represent employment affiliation concurrent with enrollment in the designated curriculum. A likely candidate for this base period designation is the full quarter before the one during which a student exited the curriculum. This two-quarter linkage will reveal three subsets of the original population whose members will be defined as job entrants for Tier 1 mandated accountability reporting purposes. Exact matches of Social Security number and employer UI tax account number pairings in the two quarters will identify those former students who were already working for the employer before leaving school; they cannot be described as job entrants in the sense of having established a new employer affiliation after leaving school. Cases in which a former student's Social Security number is paired with a different employer UI tax account number in the base quarter than in the end quarter indicate movement between employers during the observation interval. The absence of a former student's Social Security number in the base period of the linked data sets indicates that no covered employer in the state reported earnings for this person during the reference quarter.

This simple concept of segmenting job entrants into continuing employees, movers, and new appearances enriches the accountability story that can be told, even without any reference to earnings profiles. Simple graphics can be used to show differences in these percentages across curricula, or within a designated curriculum over time.

When a diagnostic refinement is undertaken, such as deconstructing the basic concept of job entry, a serious effort should be made to balance accuracy and client understanding. The circumstances of each release of accountability data are likely to dictate quite different investments in accuracy and recipient awareness. The process of calculating a performance measure value should be explained on a need-to-know basis. Two criteria should guide this decision—the risk of misunderstanding, and the expected consequences of miscommunication. The history of performance measurement offers too many examples of equally unfortunate over- and under-investments in customer understanding of released data.

Reliance on linked administrative records, without complementary information drawn from other sources, such as the surveys described in other chapters of this volume, will answer some questions. But this new limited information will trigger other questions that cannot be answered without further investigation. Seppanen describes cases in which former students do not change employer affiliation but are known to have qualified for a new assignment based on licensure or other certification. It is not easy to document reassignments of employee responsibility. This means that community college management teams will be vulnerable to allegations that relatively high rates of continuing employer affiliations indicate a possible failure to prepare students for candidacy elsewhere. Earnings data help to counter such allegations.

States that currently use earnings as a measure of performance have typically adopted one of two approaches—either add up all earnings reported using a particular Social Security number during a reference quarter, without regard to the number of reporting employers, or use the highest dollar amount reported by one of multiple reporting employers. Either approach suffices for some accountability purposes, but refinements are needed to tell a clearer story about student outcomes. We do not want to equate the circumstances of a person holding two jobs at the same time with those of someone who earns the same amount from just one job.

Seppanen correctly warns readers that Washington State is unusual in having a data element that documents hours worked during a reference quarter. Other states do not have direct access to any information about a former student's full- or part-time employment status, or awareness of when employment began during a quarter. It is beyond the intent of this chapter to describe approaches that have been taken to calculate the equivalent of full-time year-round earnings. Instead, a warning is offered. The frequency of less than full-time year-round employment is high among community college leavers. The incidence of movement among employers is also high and uneven across curricula and substate areas. There is ample and growing opportunity for oversight board members, curious students, and media representatives to misunderstand the simple earnings figures that are, or soon will be, released through mandatory performance reporting pipelines. But there are parallel opportunities to invest in less publicized diagnostics to understand more about the mix of earnings profiles that remain hidden beneath the veneer of a single composite number, such as median earnings of job entrants.

The Decision to Invest in Management Diagnostics

Too much attention will always be given by adversaries to what we are unable to measure. Accept this criticism, but place it in a quantitative context. Out-of-state employment and self-employment are difficult to measure. This may affect job entry and average earnings calculations. Acknowledge this, but seek to define the relevance of these omissions, which will not be uniform across curricula and institutions. The Tier 1 mandatory performance measures will emerge soon. These will be blunt instruments and lightning rods for dissention. They will raise the stakes for community college management teams. Those who dig deeper than before to understand more about community college employment and earnings outcomes will fare well. Those who do nothing will be exposed to new risks associated with reliance on Tier 1 performance measures alone.

So, there is no decision to be made about whether to get involved with Tier 2 opportunities. The tactical issue is whether to go it alone or join forces with others who face the same opportunities and threats. A strong case can be made for joining forces with others. A reservoir of expertise is available to help form and sustain such partnerships.

Much of what can and should be done is appropriate for state action taken in concert with local partners. The employment and earnings data are confidential and owned by a state's employment security agency. These will not be shared with individual community colleges. A central node of some sort is needed. Again, the chapters in this volume describe quite different configurations of this node. Community college management teams are involved in different ways that reflect state nuances of governance, funding flows, personalities, and historical events. No one approach is obviously best for all. But some approach will clearly trump inaction.

My advice, based on more than three decades of involvement in educational performance measurement, is to be a player. Do not sit on the sidelines frustrated with the pace and pervasiveness of change, or confident that this too shall pass with little trace of local impact. The Tier 1 performance measures will soon be on public display. I would not want to be judged by these alone. They will be an excellent place to start. They will represent genuine progress toward consumer empowerment. This is a potential threat. But it is an opportunity, too. Who will control the spin?

DAVID W. STEVENS is executive director of the Jacob France Center at the University of Baltimore.

This chapter provides an annotated bibliography of studies on the economic benefits of a community college degree. It includes national surveys and graduate surveys done at individual colleges.

Sources and Information: Economic Benefits of a Community College Degree

Elizabeth Foote

As community colleges comply with federal, state, and local demands for greater accountability, more studies of the economic benefits of a certificate or associate degree have been completed. Most report an increase in graduates' economic worth and employment rates, depending on the field of study (see both Grubb entries, below).

The materials reviewed in this chapter reflect the current ERIC literature on the economic benefits of a community college degree. These citations offer national and local surveys.

Most ERIC documents (publications with ED numbers) can be viewed on microfiche at approximately nine hundred libraries worldwide. In addition, most may be ordered on microfiche or on paper copy from the ERIC Document Reproduction Service (EDRS) at (800) 443–ERIC. Citations preceded by an asterisk (*) refer to journal articles that are not available from EDRS. Journal articles may be acquired through regular library channels or purchased from one of the following article reproduction services: Carl Uncover: http://www.carl.org/uncover/, uncover@carl.org, (800)787–7979; UMI: orders@infostore.com, (800) 248–0360; or ISI: tga@isinet.com, (800) 523–1850.

General Articles

Constantine, Jill M., and Neumark, David. *Training and the Growth of Wage Inequality. EQW Working Papers WP31.* Philadelphia, Pa.: National Center on the Educational Quality of the Workforce, 1994. 31 pp. (ED 394 000)

The relationship between training and the growth in wage inequality was examined through an analysis of data from the January 1983 and January 1991 supplements to the Current Population Survey. The analysis focused on whether the distribution of training has changed in ways that may explain changes in the wage structure during the period studied and whether the changes in training, combined with the effects of training on wages, are sufficiently large to have induced the changes in wage structure observed during the 1980s. The shifts in the incidence in the various types of training offered during the 1980s were found to favor more educated, more experienced workers. When the observed shifts were considered in conjunction with the fact that training is associated with higher wages, it was concluded that training may have contributed to the growth of wage inequality during the 1980s. Further analysis established, however, that training did not play any substantial role in the increase in wage inequality observed during the 1980s. It was hypothesized that either the shifts in training distribution were too small or the returns on training were too low for training to have been a major factor in increased wage inequality.

Crawford, David L., Johnson, Amy W., and Summers, Anita A. *Schools and Labor Market Outcomes. EQW Working Papers WP33.* Philadelphia, Pa.: National Center on the Educational Quality of the Workforce, 1995. 38 pp. (ED 394 002)

The relationship between school characteristics and labor market outcomes was examined through a literature review and an econometric analysis of the effects of various characteristics of the schooling experience on students' labor market performance after high school. Data from the National Center on Education Statistics' longitudinal survey of students (*High School and Beyond,* 1980), were subjected to a number of regressions that used two different models. It was discovered that schools make a difference in the labor market performance of those graduates who enter the labor market directly after high school. Particular characteristics were identified as affecting earnings; however, the aggregation of the school characteristics assembled did not decisively explain differences in the job market performance. Attendance of a school where up-to-date local job listings were available and information on finding a job was provided, higher family income, higher school test scores, and participation in academic education were all linked with higher postschool earnings, whereas per-pupil expenditure, class size, teacher salaries, and teacher experience were not. (Appended are the following: summary of relevant studies, sources/definitions of variables, means and standard deviations for variables used in the regressions, and the two models.)

Ghazalah, I. A. *1984 Vocational Education Graduates in 1988. A Study Based on Federal Income Tax Data.* Athens: Ohio University, 1993. 130 pp. (ED 367 806)

A 1988 study that examined the economic performance of 22,091 graduates in 1984 of fourteen vocational programs in Ohio used federal income tax records. Twelve of the programs with 20,557 graduates were at the secondary level, and two with 1,534 graduates were at the associate level. The incomes of vocational graduates were compared to incomes of equivalent groups in the general population. The study also investigated the geographic mobility of vocational graduates since 1979. Results showed predominantly higher incomes for vocational graduates than for the general population. The result varied by vocational program, but the ratios were higher than 1 for the 1979 graduates in all programs. The income advantage ranged from 5 to 85 percent for graduates of secondary programs and from 12 to 68 percent for graduates of associate programs.

Hollenbeck, Kevin. "Postsecondary Education as Triage: Returns to Academic and Technical Programs." Staff Working Papers 92–10. Kalamazoo, Mich.: Upjohn (W.E.) Institute for Employment Research, 1992. 38 pp. (ED 381 687). (Paper copy not available from EDRS; order from W. E. Upjohn Institute for Employment Research, 300 South Westnedge Avenue, Kalamazoo, MI 49007; $2)
　　A study evaluated the labor market outcomes of individuals with various types of postsecondary educational experiences. In particular, it examined differences among three groups: students who pursued technical education programs; those who pursued academic programs; and those individuals who did not pursue any type of postsecondary education. The study used empirical evidence from the National Longitudinal Survey of High School Students in 1972 concerning the relationship between economic outcomes and grades earned and the degree to which the labor market rewarded credentials. Wages and earning models yielded different structural parameter estimates when based on the three populations. The differences were most dramatic for high school background effects and for postsecondary characteristics. The empirical results from the technique used to correct for self-selection suggested that individuals' choices among the three postsecondary tracks were not the result of absolute advantage.

Senate Committee on Labor and Human Resources. *Education's Impact on Economic Competitiveness.* Hearing on Examining Education's Impact on Economic Competitiveness before the Subcommittee on Education, Arts and Humanities of the Committee on Labor and Human Resources. United States Senate, One Hundred Fourth Congress, First Session. Washington, D.C.: Senate Committee on Labor and Human Resources, 1995. 121 pp. (ED 382 862). (Also available from U.S. Government Printing Office, Superintendent of Documents, Congressional Sales Office, Washington, D.C. 20402) ·
　　This document contains the text of testimony presented at a congressional hearing examining education's role in economic competitiveness. Senator James M. Jefford's opening statement is followed by testimony given by representatives of the following agencies and organizations: TRW, Inc., Circuit City Stores, Inc., McGraw-Hill, Inc., Drew University, U.S. Bureau of the Census, University of Southern California, Cornell University, and Knowledge Network for All Americans. Also included is a contribution titled "Improving Education:

How Large Are the Benefits? How Can It Be Done Efficiently?" (Bishop), and a contribution titled "Improving National Economic Competitiveness through Educational Investment" (Lloyd). Charts summarizing the following are contained in the testimony: average annual federal taxes by family for 1991, change in median family income by education, education loan debt, employment by major economic sector from 1800 to 1993, the growing gap between individuals based on mastery of the skills required for economic competitiveness, distribution of available capital stocks in the U.S. business economy, components fueling domestic economic growth in the United States from 1929 to 1990, and shifts in federal budget priorities from 1993 to 1995.

"Starting Salaries of College Graduates. Indicator of the Month." Washington, D.C.: National Center for Education Statistics, 1997. 4 pp. (ED 409 786)
    This brief summary report provides data on differences in starting salaries of college graduates and the related changing demands of the labor market. The report notes that (1) between 1977 and 1993 computer sciences and engineering graduates had much higher starting salaries than graduates in all other fields of study; (2) although starting salaries for humanities and education graduates have varied over time, generally they were considerably lower than starting salaries for all graduates; (3) among 1993 graduates females were more likely than males to major in education, and males were more likely than females to major in computer sciences and engineering; (4) the most common field of study for both males and females was business; and (5) median starting salaries for 1993 male graduates were higher than those for females. Two tables provide data for percentage differences between median starting salaries for all graduates versus graduates in particular fields of study for the years 1977–1993, and annual median starting salaries of 1993 graduates by sex and major field of study. Starting salaries of college graduates by field of discipline are graphed.

National Surveys

Several projects have researched the economic benefit of a community college degree on a national level. The following articles are a sample.

Grubb, W. Norton. *The Returns to Education and Training in the Sub-Baccalaureate Labor Market: Evidence from the Survey of Income and Program Participation 1984–1990.* Berkeley, Calif.: National Center for Research in Vocational Education, 1995. 80 pp. (ED 382 839). (Also available from NCRVE Materials Distribution Service, Horrabin Hall 46, Western Illinois University, Macomb, IL 61455; order no. MDS–765: $5)
    The Survey of Income and Program Participation (SIPP) was used to compare estimates of the benefits of education among different levels of education and thereby identify the returns to education and training in the sub-baccalaureate labor market. The study data consisted of information on

the educational attainment and income of 14,537 (7,981 males; 6,556 females), 10,384 (5,452 males; 4,952 females), and 20,539 (10,600 males; 9,939 females) SIPP respondents (aged twenty-five to sixty-four years) for calendar years 1984, 1987, and 1990, respectively. Estimating equations describing respondents' earnings as a function of education and other conventional independent variables were constructed, and the results were analyzed. Both certificates and associate degrees were found to increase the earnings of those who received them, albeit not by as much as a baccalaureate degree does. Some kinds of postsecondary education provided no economic advantage at all, and completion of a certificate proved more beneficial than completion of years of college without a credential. As is the case for baccalaureate degrees, the benefits of sub-baccalaureate credentials varied substantially by field of study, and the effects of having a job related to one's field of study proved substantial. Sixteen tables are included. Information about the samples and selected independent variables and a field-of-study/occupation-matching algorithm are appended. Contains forty-four references.

*Grubb, W. Norton. "Postsecondary Education and the Sub-Baccalaureate Labor Market: Corrections and Extensions." *Economics of Education Review,* 1995, *14* (3), 285–299.
    Corrects 1972 National Longitudinal Study data used in two earlier papers on education effects in sub-baccalaureate labor markets. Corrections confirm most earlier findings. However, for men, the effects of vocational associate degrees are insignificant, whereas the effects of vocational credits earned are significant. Economic benefits may accrue to small amounts of community college.

*Leigh, Duane E., and Gill, Andrew M. "Labor Market Returns to Community Colleges: Evidence for Returning Adults." *Journal of Human Resources,* 1997, *32* (2), 334–353.
    Analysis of National Longitudinal Survey of Youth samples shows that for both associate degree and nondegree community college programs, returning adults experience the same earnings increases as continuing high school graduates. Returning males in nondegree programs receive an earnings effect 8 to 10 percent above that of continuing students.

Stevens, David W. *The School-to-Work Transition of High School and Community College Vocational Program Completers: 1990–1992.* EQW Working Papers WP27. Philadelphia, Penn.: National Center on the Educational Quality of the Workforce, 1994. 114 pp. (ED 393 997)
    The school-to-work transition of high school and community college vocational program completers in 1990–1992 was examined by analyzing administrative records and employment and earnings data of vocational program completers from state education agencies in Colorado, Florida, Missouri, and Washington. A consistently high percentage of vocational program completers

at both the high school and postsecondary levels continued an uninterrupted affiliation with the same employer during the bridge period encompassing their last months in school and first few months after leaving school; however, substantial movement between/among employers during the first years after the former students left school was observed. Former students who continued with the same employer through the bridge period were consistently found to have higher earnings than their classmates while they were still in school, shortly after leaving school, and at the end of the postschool reference period. It was concluded that knowledge about a former student's occupational assignment within a place of employment is not needed to predict that employee's earnings; rather, awareness of the person's industry affiliation is an acceptable substitute for that purpose. (Forty tables and figures and eighty-six endnotes are included. Appended are additional information on the wage-record components examined and calculation of a full-time earnings threshold amount.)

Single College Surveys

The following articles present findings and analysis from studies done at individual community colleges.

Community College of Rhode Island. *Career Placement and Graduate Transfer Report, 1996.* Warwick: Community College of Rhode Island, 1997. 56 pp. (ED 409 966)

This report provides data on the career and transfer outcomes of 1996 graduates from the Community College of Rhode Island (CCRI). A brief foreword indicates that surveys were distributed to 1,669 graduates from 1996, with 82.7 percent (n=1,381) responding. Next, data on graduate outcomes are presented for the following twenty-seven programs: business administration, cardiorespiratory care, chemical technology, clinical laboratory technology, computer studies, criminal justice and legal studies, dental assistant, dental hygiene, electronics, engineering, engineering technology, fine arts, fire science, human services, liberal arts, machine design, manufacturing technology, nursing (associate degree), nursing (licensed practical), office administration, phlebotomy, physical therapist assistant, process control technology, radiography, retail management, science, and technical studies. For each program, information is provided on the number of responding graduates, percentages of graduates employed or continuing their education, average salaries of employed graduates, graduate employers (including the number of graduates employed by each), and receiving colleges, including the number of graduates enrolled by major. Highlighted findings indicate that 85.7 percent of the graduates were employed, with 53.3 percent working full-time; and that 36.9 percent were continuing their education, with 28.5 percent of these attending school full-time. Appendixes provide a list of CCRI programs and concentrations, the survey instrument, graphs of placement and transfer outcomes, and a comparison of 1994, 1995, and 1996 graduates.

Illinois Community College Board. *Occupational Program Graduates 1997 Follow-Up Study.* Springfield, Ill.: Illinois Community College Board, 1997. 72 pp. (ED 411 922)

This report provides information from graduates of selected occupational programs regarding the effectiveness of their Illinois community college experience, addressing issues such as employment status and satisfaction of employment and components of the educational program completed. A total of 3,578 former students who graduated from forty selected Illinois community college programs in fiscal year 1996 were surveyed in March 1997, approximately six to nine months after program completion. Study findings, based on responses from 2,070 graduates in thirty-six program areas, included the following: (1) 92.7 percent were employed or pursuing additional education or both; (2) 89 percent of the occupational completers were employed, with 81.2 percent working in positions related to their training; (3) 82.2 percent of the employed graduates had full-time status; (4) 18.8 percent of graduates were working in positions unrelated to their area of training; (5) the average hourly salary for full- and part-time employed graduates was $11.47; (6) on average, graduates ranked their degree of satisfaction with the program at 4.13 on a 5–point scale; and (7) 25 percent of the respondents were pursuing additional education. An analysis of outcomes for thirty-seven programs is included. Data tables showing response rates and outcomes by college and by selected occupational programs are appended.

Luan, Jing. *Using Wage Record Data to Measure the Success of Students in the Labor Market: A Longitudinal Study of Former Cabrillo College Occupational Education Students' Employment and Wages (Cohorts 1990 and 1991).* Aptos, Calif.: Cabrillo College, 1996. 25 pp. (ED 405 938)

In 1995, Cabrillo College was one of eighteen California community colleges to participate in a pilot study on the uses of unemployment insurance (UI) wage record data for tracking employment rates of former community college students. The employment status of students who left the college in 1990 and 1991 was reported for their last year in college, first year out of college, and third year out of college. Data were collected by linking student records available through the statewide Management Information System with UI wage records maintained in the Employment Development Department. Results included the following: (1) of the 17,115 students in the study, UI wage record data were available for 77 percent of the students in the year they last attended college, 74 percent of the students in their first year after leaving college, and 67 percent of the students in their third year after college; (2) for students under twenty-five years of age, the largest gain in salary (123.7 percent) occurred among students who had obtained a certificate or associate degree; (3) of the twelve majors studied, students in the fire protection, radiological technology, nursing, dental hygiene, electronic technology, computer science, and business programs earned over $20,000 their first year out of college; and (4) in the first year out of college, Latinos who completed a degree or certificate earned $29,071, compared to $22,664 for noncompleting Latinos.

Saint Petersburg Junior College, Office of Institutional Research. *The Graduate Survey, 1992–93.* St. Petersburg, Fla: Saint Petersburg Junior College, 1995. 56 pp. (ED 391 544)

In 1994, St. Petersburg Junior College (SPJC), in Florida, conducted a survey to determine the level of satisfaction with programs and services among graduates from 1992–1993, the extent that graduates achieved their goals, and factors affecting goal achievement. Telephone and mail surveys resulted in responses from 1,358 of the 2,595 1992–1993 graduates. An analysis of responses revealed the following: (1) 85.7 percent of the graduates felt that their overall experience at SPJC was very valuable or somewhat valuable, and 83.4 percent were very or somewhat satisfied with programs and services; (2) over 92 percent of the respondents indicated that they had achieved their goal; (3) of the 66 percent of graduates attending a four-year college, 94 percent had associate of arts (AA) degrees and 55 percent reported enrolling in the same major as at SPJC; (4) 79 percent of the graduates reported that they were employed, with 92.1 percent of associate of science (AS) and 75.1 percent of AA graduates indicating that they worked; (5) AS graduates employed full-time had higher income earnings than AA graduates, with annual salaries averaging over $30,000; (6) 92.7 percent of the AS graduates were working in their preferred field; and (7) although graduates with higher grade point averages had higher rates of goal achievement, no student demographic characteristics were found to be related to achievement. The survey instrument, response rates by program, and student comments are appended.

Spartanburg Technical College, Office of Institutional Research. *Spartanburg Technical College 1987–1988 Graduates: 3-Year Follow-Up Study. Summary of Report.* Spartanburg, S.C.: Spartanburg Technical College, 1991. 28 pp. (ED 410 985)

In June 1991, a study was conducted at South Carolina's Spartanburg Technical College to determine the career and educational experiences of graduates who had received an associate degree, diploma, or certificate in the 1987–1988 academic year. Surveys were sent to 354 graduates, resulting in 123 usable responses. Study findings included the following: (1) 34 percent of the respondents were male, 10 percent were members of minority groups, and 45 percent were between twenty-one and twenty-five years of age; (2) 42.4 percent of the respondents had indicated upon enrollment that their main objective was to learn skills to enter the job market; (3) 94.5 percent indicated that they had achieved their main objective while enrolled at the college; (4) 94.3 percent were employed or continuing their education; (5) 81.3 percent of the employed respondents were in jobs related to their area of studies; (6) 20.8 percent indicated that they earned over $26,000 per year, and 16 percent had gross annual incomes of $14,000 or less; and (7) 77.6 percent agreed that the college provided either excellent or good preparation for employment. Tables of responses, including a chart of employers by college program, are included. The survey instrument is appended.

ELIZABETH FOOTE is the user services coordinator at the ERIC Clearinghouse for Community Colleges.

INDEX

AACC. *See* American Association of Community Colleges

Accountability, institutional: external reporting requirements in, 95, 96; federally mandated, 11, 41-42; historical concepts of, 10; state-mandated, 11, 65–66. *See also* Performance measures

Adams, W., 6

American Association of Community Colleges (AACC), core indicators of program effectiveness, 12–13, 55

Anderberg, M., 9, 90, 92

Astin, A. W., 7, 10

Baccalaureate degree, community college education and, 7, 85, 91

Banta, T. W., 10

Becker, G. S., 6

Bellevue Community College (BCC), workforce initiative of: collaboration in, 62–63, 64–65; curriculum development in, 62; data limitations in, 65–66; and high-wage program development, 63–65; and new program marketing and recruitment, 64–65; and regional technology workforce shortage, 61–62; and state accountability measures, 65–66

Bogue, G., 53

Boyer, C. M., 10

Bragg, D., 91

Brawer, F. B., 4

Brayson, D. D., 56

Brown, K., 57

Building a Foundation for Tomorrow: Skill Standards for Information Technology, 62–63

Caffrey, J., 70

California community colleges: enrollment statistics, 77; reporting requirements, 41; state wage data use by, 71–72; and state-mandated accountability, 11. *See also* Southwestern College

California Community Colleges Chancellor's Office Management Information System (COMIS) database, 42–47, 71–72, 78

California community colleges, post-college earnings studies, 77–86; adjustment of earnings in, 79–80; collaboration in, 44–49; COMIS and UI database linkage in, 43–47; consolidation of program outcomes in, 48; cost-effectiveness in, 84; data limitations in, 44, 45–46, 79; data-matching system development in, 44–50; EDD staff involvement in, 49; EDD-UI and MIS data matching in, 78; feasibility study in, 43–47; methodology development in, 44–49; policy and practice implications of, 50, 86; and privacy regulations, 47, 49–50; problems of aggregating outcomes in, 48; statewide findings of, 80–86; student categorization in, 79; systemwide implementation of, 47–48; tracking system in, 78–79

Career Placement and Graduate Transfer Report, 108

Carl D. Perkins Vocational and Applied Technology Education Act, 89–90; accountability mandate of, 11, 41–42; amendments to, 92, 95; collaborative requirements in, 42–43; core performance requirements in, 20

Carvell, F., 69

Certification, 7

Cohen, A. M., 4

Constantine, J. M., 103

Crawford, D. L., 104

Creech, J., 53

Data, aggregate: cost-effectiveness of, 84; creation of new knowledge from, 29, 33–37; limitations and benefits of, 86; public access to, 47, 49–50, 96

Data Linking for Outcomes Assessment (DLOA): aggregation of results in, 38; creation of, 30–31; data-related design choices in, 37–38; employment rate and wage information in, 33–35; indexing of quarters in, 37; inflation-adjusted data in, 38; policy issues related to, 39; pre- and post-training earnings comparisons in, 38; and program difference in potential earnings, 35–36; testing value-add of college in, 36–37; user-friendly format of, 31–32

Develop a Curriculum (DACUM) process, 62

Eaton, J., 5
Economic benefits of community college education, 93–94; comparative, 7–8; defined, 6; surveys and studies on, 106–110. *See also* Post-college earnings analysis
Education's Impact on Economic Competitiveness, 105–106
Employer screening, 7
Erzen, R., 70
Ewell, P. T., 10

Family Education Rights and Privacy Act (FERPA), 47, 49
Florida Education and Training Placement Information Program (FETPIP), 9, 19, 20, 21, 24
Florida higher education: comparative post-college earnings in, 17; and performance measurement waiver plan, 21; and Performance-Based Incentive Funding, 23–24; and Performance-Based Program Budgeting, 24; placement performance requirement in, 19; and S.B.1688 (workforce education program fund), 24–27
Florida workforce development system, 17–28; consolidation of performance measures in, 20–23; core components of, 18; federal requirements in, 20; funding of, 19, 23–27; interagency data collection system in, 19, 20; measurement tools of, 18–19; performance output/outcome measures in, 25; and welfare reform initiative, 21; and Workforce Florida Act, 21–23
Folger, J., 53
Foote, E., 103
Friedlander, J., 11, 44, 45, 47, 77, 92
Froeschle, R., 43, 77
Funding, performance-based, 12, 23–27, 95–96

Gaither, G., 53
Ghazalah, I. A., 104
Gill, A. M., 107
Gracie, L. W., 53
Graham, M., 69
Grubb, W. N., 6, 7, 8, 34, 85, 91, 106, 107

Haenn, J. F., 44
Haller, A., 6

Henderson, C., 6
High-wage program development, 61–67
Hollenbeck, K., 105
Human capital theory, 6–8
Hutchison, K. R., 61

Institutional effectiveness, assessment of, 54, 73–75
Issacs, H., 70

Jaffe, A., 6
Jencks, C., 7
Johnson, A. W., 104

Kane, T., 34
Kline, S. S., 61, 90
Koltai, L., 5

Laanan, F. S., 5, 6, 77, 84, 91
Leigh, D. E., 107
Length of schooling, and socialization hypothesis, 85
Luan, J., 109

MacDougall, P. R., 11
Management diagnostics: accountability reporting for, 95, 96–100; earnings analysis for, 91, 92
Mandt, C., 61
Marks, J. L., 53
Marks, S., 61
Measure, defined, 90
Medrich, E., 90
Michie, J. S., 44

Neal, J. E., 53
Nedwek, B. P., 53
Neumark, D., 103
1984 Vocational Education Graduates in 1988, 104–105
North Carolina higher education system: Annual Programs Review, 55–56; community college governance, 54; development of accountability standards in, 54–55; educational and economic development policies in, 54–55
North Carolina workforce development efforts: and Common Follow-up Management Information System (CFS), 9, 54, 56, 59; and Critical Success Factors, 55; data analysis and findings in, 57; and development of longitudinal data-

base, 59–60; policy implications of, 60; reporting system of, 53, 55–56; and return on investment, 56; and state workforce development programs, 56; unemployment insurance data in, 56
Northwest Center for Emerging Technologies (NWCET), 62–63, 64

Ottinger, C., 6
Outcalt, C., 11
Outcome, defined, 89–90

Pascarella, E., 85
Performance measurement: AACC recommendations for, 12–13; accuracy and recipient awareness issues in, 99; and aggregation of individualized student outcome measures, 90; implications of using aggregate earnings data in, 86; for management diagnostics, 91, 92, 95, 96–100; mandated, 10–11, 89–90, 96; and placement rate in workforce, 12; set of core indicators in, 12–13; state survey of, 11–12; state systems of, 53, 92–93; types of, 11; uniform criteria development, 90
Performance-based funding, 12, 23–27, 95–96
Perkins Act. See Carl D. Perkins Vocational and Applied Technical Education Act
Pfeiffer, J. J., 9, 17, 43, 90, 92
Piland, W. E., 69, 70, 71
Post-college earnings analysis: and accountability reporting for management diagnostics, 95, 96–100; administrative databases in, 42–43; assessment methodology in, 8–10; collaboration in, 42–43, 93; comparative findings on, 93–94; creation of new knowledge in, 29, 33–37; data limitations in, 50, 86; and economic benefits of community college education, 6–8; and educational attainment, 6–8; and external reporting requirements, 95, 96; through follow-up surveys, 43; job entry and average earnings calculations in, 98–100; local research efforts in, 91–92; and national measurement efforts, 92–94; and national regulations, 89–91; performance funding incentives in, 95–96; program-level, 91, 92; public access to, 92, 96; research findings on, 91–92; and return on investment, 92–93; state man-

agement of, 96–97; student records and unemployment insurance database linkage in, 43–44; unemployment insurance (UI) wage data in, 91, 96, 98. See also specific college; state initiative
Post-Education Employment Tracking System (PEETS), 78–79
Privacy considerations, 47, 49–50
Program evaluation and improvement: and development of high-wage employment, 61–67; federal policy on, 89–91; post-college wage data in, 54–56, 75; statewide outcome-based framework for, 92

Rabin, J., 11
Regional Advanced Technology Education Consortium (RATEC), 62, 63, 64
Richmond, P. A., 44
Romano, R. M., 6
Rouse, C. E., 34
Ryan, J., 70

Sanchez, J. R., 5, 6, 84, 89, 91
Schools and Labor Market Outcomes, 104
School-to-Work Transition of High School and Community College Vocational Program Completers: 1990–1992, 107
Seppanen, L. J., 8, 9, 10, 29, 33, 43, 77
Shi, J., 91
Smith, A., 89
Southwestern College: local economy impact of, 70–71; and state wage findings and utilization, 73–75; student body characteristics, 69–70
Spartanburg Technical College, 110
Special populations, short-term programs for, 85–86
Standard, defined, 90
State Higher Education Executive Officers (SHEEO), 11–12
Stecher, B., 89
Stevens, D. W., 31, 44, 91, 95, 107
Student outcomes analysis. See Post-college earnings analysis
Student Right to Know Act, 41
Summers, A. A., 104
Survey of Income and Program Participation (SIPP), 7

Terenzini, P., 85
Texas, automated student follow-up in, 9–10

Texas State Occupational Information Coordinating Committee (SOICC), 10
Toward Establishing a Unified System of Performance Measures, 90
Training and the Growth of Wage Inequality, 103–104

Unemployment insurance (UI) wage data, 8–10, 38–39, 96; as core database, 90, 91; deficiencies in, 50, 86; elements of, 98; and public disclosure, 92; similarity of, across states, 44, 91. *See also* Data Linking for Outcomes Assessment (DLOA)
U.S. Bureau of the Census, 71
U.S. Department of Education, 11
U.S. Department of Labor, 6, 62
U.S. Job Training Partnership Act, 20
U.S. Senate Committee on Labor and Human Resources, 105

Vanderheyden, B., 9, 77
Vocational-technical education: account-

ability requirements for, 11; foundation of, 5, 7; and transfer rates to four-year colleges, 91. *See also* Post-college earnings analysis

Washington State workforce development: automated data-linking system in, 10, 29, 30–39; and community and technical college system, 29–30; development of high-wage programs in, 61–67; partnership efforts in, 30; responses to accountability and measurement requirements in, 65–66; and State Board for Community and Technical Colleges (SBCTC), 29, 30–31, 32. *See also* Bellevue Community College; Data Linking for Outcomes Assessment (DLOA)
Welfare-to-work programs, 21, 39, 85
Westat, Inc., 35
Wiseley, W. C., 41
Workforce Investment Act, 95

Yang, X., 57

Back Issue/Subscription Order Form

Copy or detach and send to:
Jossey-Bass Inc., Publishers, 350 Sansome Street, San Francisco CA 94104-1342

Call or fax toll free!
Phone 888-378-2537 6AM-5PM PST; Fax 800-605-2665

Back issues: Please send me the following issues at $25 each
(Important: please include series initials and issue number, such as CC90)

1. CC _____

_____

_____

$ _____ Total for single issues

$ _____ Shipping charges (for single issues *only;* subscriptions are exempt
from shipping charges): Up to $30, add $5^{50} • $30^{01}–$50, add $6^{50}
$50^{01}–$75, add $7^{50} • $75^{01}–$100, add $9 • $100^{01}–$150, add $10
Over $150, call for shipping charge

Subscriptions   Please ❑ start   ❑ renew my subscription to *New Directions
for Community Colleges* for the year 19___ at the following rate:

    ❑ Individual $57   ❑ Institutional $107
NOTE: Subscriptions are quarterly, and are for the calendar year only.
Subscriptions begin with the spring issue of the year indicated above.
For shipping outside the U.S., please add $25.

$ _____ Total single issues and subscriptions (CA, IN, NJ, NY and DC
residents, add sales tax for single issues. NY and DC residents must
include shipping charges when calculating sales tax. NY and Canadian
residents only, add sales tax for subscriptions)

❑ Payment enclosed (U.S. check or money order only)
❑ VISA, MC, AmEx, Discover Card # _____ Exp. date _____

Signature _____ Day phone _____
❑ Bill me (U.S. institutional orders only. Purchase order required)
Purchase order # _____

Name _____
Address _____

_____

Phone_____ E-mail _____

For more information about Jossey-Bass Publishers, visit our Web site at:
www.josseybass.com   **PRIORITY CODE = ND1**

CC103   Creating and Benefiting from Institutional Collaboration: Models for Success,
        Dennis McGrath
CC102   Organizational Change in the Community College: A Ripple or a Sea Change?
        John Stewart Levin
CC101   Integrating Technology on Campus: Human Sensibilities and Technical
        Possibilities, *Kamala Anandam*
CC100   Implementing Effective Policies for Remedial and Developmental Education,
        Jan M. Ignash
CC99   Building a Working Policy for Distance Education, *Connie L. Dillon, Rosa
        Cintrón*
CC98   Presidents and Trustees in Partnership: New Roles and Leadership Challenges,
        Iris M. Weisman, George B. Vaughan
CC97   School-to-Work Systems: The Role of Community Colleges in Preparing
        Students and Facilitating Transitions, *Edgar I. Farmer, Cassy B. Key*
CC96   Transfer and Articulation: Improving Policies to Meet New Needs, *Tronie Rifkin*
CC95   Graduate and Continuing Education for Community College Leaders: What It
        Means Today, *James C. Palmer, Stephen G. Katsinas*
CC94   Achieving Administrative Diversity, *Raymond C. Bowen, Gilbert H. Muller*
CC93   Promoting Community Renewal Through Civic Literacy and Service Learning,
        Michael H. Parsons, David C. Lisman
CC92   Curriculum Models for General Education, *George Higginbottom, Richard M.
        Romano*
CC91   Community Colleges and Proprietary Schools: Conflict or Convergence? *Darrel
        A. Clowes, Elizabeth M. Hawthorne*
CC90   Portrait of the Rural Community College, *Jim Killacky, James R. Valadez*
CC89   Gender and Power in the Community College, *Barbara K. Townsend*
CC82   Academic Advising: Organizing and Delivering Services for Student Success,
        Margaret C. King
CC77   Critical Thinking: Educational Imperative, *Cynthia A. Barnes*